Beth Russell's TRADITIONAL NEEDLEPOINT

Beth Russell's TRADITIONAL NEEDLEPOINT

Photography by
JOHN GREENWOOD

*My work is the embodiment of dreams
in one form or another . . .*
WILLIAM MORRIS, 1856

David & Charles

For Peter, Nick and Sam,
Paul and Julie

A DAVID & CHARLES BOOK

First published in the UK in 1992, reprinted 1993
First paperback edition 1999, reprinted 2003

Distributed in North America
by F&W Publications, Inc.
4700 East Galbraith Road
Cincinnati, OH 45236
1-800-289-0963

A catalogue record for this book is available from the
British Library.

ISBN 0 7153 0960 9 paperback

Printed in China by Midas Printing International Ltd
On behalf of Compass Press Limited
for David & Charles Brunel House Newton Abbot Devon

CONTENTS

INTRODUCTION

EMBROIDERY IS A WAY of life for me – it is both my work and my joy. It can be a wonderful source of companionship, sharing and comparing experiences and experiments with friends. At times it can be so totally absorbing that being alone is a pleasure.

Driving home on a bleak day is one of the times that I most relish the thought of returning to my stitching. The anticipation of a warm room, a cosy chair and a challenging design cancels all the frustrations of the day. As I make the first stitch, all the thoughts, dreams, hopes and happenings of the previous stitching flood my mind as if they were woven into the embroidery itself and are once again released.

Beth Russell as a child in Welsh costume.

•

A WELSH CHILDHOOD

Memories of my life as a young girl in South Wales conjure up feelings of complete security: a calm, kind mother, a warm welcoming kitchen smelling of fresh-baked bread, coal fires, freezing bathrooms, back doors that were never locked, popping into neighbours' homes for tea and Welsh cakes. Security meant feeling totally free to run in the fields . . . climb fences, trees, hills . . . and spend hours underneath a wheelbarrow waiting for the rain to see if my makeshift 'house' was waterproof. In the evenings, I would watch my father paint in oils or watercolours, make furniture, satchels and even shoes; at Christmas he made the best consommé I've ever tasted. I shared a private world of creativity within the home, complemented by the freedom to explore the world outside.

Much has happened since then, but I think the emotional freedom that I had as a child gave me the confidence to experiment. My own methods tend to be somewhat unconventional: my instinct is to try something first and take lessons later. However, in this book, I offer the best technical advice that I can find from experts. This, combined with my enthusiasm for experimentation, will hopefully furnish you with some of the tools to embark on your own projects. My reluctance to give instructions for certain things, such as upholstering, is not because I have never tried it, but because my methods are rather individual and, I am quite sure, not always the easiest! Although I retain the desire to explore and to challenge my own abilities, I still seek to retain the creative perfection that my father cherished.

LIFE ON THE THAMES

My present location is far away from my beginnings. These days I live high up, overlooking the River Thames, and my days are dominated by the sun. In the winter it rises and sets within our line of vision and when it shines, it stays with us all day.

My 'second' family lives here in this urban environment, so they are not blessed with the freedom that I had. However, we are compensated by the space we see, the variety of our careers and the common interests that we share.

Every member of my family has a role in our company, Designers Forum. My husband Peter, my sons Nick and Paul and my daughter-in-law Julie take care of the business side. My brother Roy Haynes gives us sound business advice, and my other daughter-in-law Sam pops in to lend a hand when we need her.

I am left free to indulge my addiction for new designs. My time may be spent drawing, colouring, visiting libraries and museums. Whenever we can, Peter and I travel to one of the famous William Morris or De Morgan houses which are such sources of inspiration. I may need to go to one of my stitchers to see how a sample is coming along. However much preliminary stitching I have done, the work tends to be rather like a scrapbook or sketch pad, and only when the parts of the design are seen in their relevant places, surrounded by background, can the true effect be judged. Every day I try to stitch a little myself, checking how colours blend together and how subtle shapes can be formed and brought to life on a rigid medium such as canvas.

I always have a stack of new designs either in my head or half-drawn or partly stitched. My itch to try the latest design in a new colourway, or with a different background, or to a different scale – before the first sample has even been completed – sometimes makes it difficult to concentrate on one thing at a time.

I love the family feeling of what I do, not only working with my immediate family, but also enjoying close friendship and helpful advice from many people who are more experienced in draughtsmanship and needlepoint than I and who are brilliant technicians who interpret my ideas into such beautiful reality.

•

Working on African Marigold, in my London studio.

DESIGNERS FORUM

From the outset I wanted Designers Forum to gain a reputation for excellence and quality. The source of my work comes from arguably the richest period in the history of British design, both in the number of great designers and the brilliance of their workmanship. My aim is to remain true to the essence of their designs, even though I change the medium with which to display them. My firm belief is that it is foolish to work with inferior materials; my father's voice saying 'If a job is worth doing, it's worth doing well' was heard too frequently for me not to believe it. Time and creativity are more valuable than the canvas and threads, and should not be wasted working with materials that will neither do justice to your efforts nor last long enough to hand down to your grandchildren.

So all Designers Forum kits contain the best canvas that we can find and are hand-printed by a perfectionist craftsman. The superb colour selection of the Appleton's range of wool provides a wealth of choice with which to echo the designs I love.

THE JOY OF STITCHERY

If you have never felt the secret joy of watching your design grow and evolve as you work, then I hope that this book will persuade you either to start stitching or – if you have already – to enjoy it even more. You will hopefully find not just designs to copy, but ideas to inspire. Once you are thoroughly involved with stitching, you can stretch your talents to the full – your sense of colour, style and texture, your ability to shade and shape – you should feel confident and

*The Pomegranate rug. Its variety
of background colours and lovely curves are typical of
William Morris's work.*

•

*The Jackfield Rose design shown
in tent stitch for a picture , and in
cross stitch for a tablecloth.*

•

free to interpret as you wish, to show what you genuinely see. You will be surprised as you unlock these hidden talents. New worlds of colour and shape will unfold. Stitching, like music or painting, involves a flow and a rhythm which are both personal and universal, creating a therapeutic peacefulness.

We all see things slightly differently; colour particularly affects us all in different ways. It is constantly fascinating to see how quickly some people can choose colours to blend and harmonise. This gift can, to a certain extent, be learned.

The more frequently colour decisions are made, the easier they become.

In this book I try to show the enormous variety of uses to which charts can be put. By changing the materials used – the gauge of canvas, the type of stitch, the colours – you will find that the same design allows you to produce an enormous number of beautiful and quite different works of art. Part of a design can be used for a single delicate picture; a cushion can be enlarged into a rug, or a rug can be reduced to a cushion. What is shown or discussed should be just the start of your experiments with charts. I hope to show the way – you can then exercise your own inspiration, tastes and needs to move ahead into your own world of artistry.

I hope that this book will prove not just the key to a door, but more a travel guide to the unexplored continent of your own abilities.

*. . . never forget the material you are working with, and try always to
use it for what it can do best . . .*
WILLIAM MORRIS (1893)

THE ARTS & CRAFTS MOVEMENT

A small section of the wallhanging embroidered by Morris himself in 1857. It is stitched in wool on linen, using a relatively unknown and difficult stitch which we are told Morris was determined to master. The original now hangs in Kelmscott Manor.

•

MY FASCINATION with the designs of William Morris remains intact after many years. The more familiar I become with them, the more enthusiastic I feel. His aims in life and in work were impeccable and his creativity seems to have been infectious. Every so often, history reports on groups of close friends who were renowned for their talents, but seldom can there have been a group displaying such a range of skills – all of a style, all complementary, yet all so individual – as the Arts & Crafts Movement. The artist Dante Gabriel Rossetti, the painter Edward Burne-Jones, the architect Philip Webb and William De Morgan, the designer of ceramics and stained glass, remained lifelong friends of Morris. Many others throughout the world also helped to provide us with the wealth of controversial yet enduring designs that were created during this period.

It is interesting to learn how the paths of so many gifted men, in this time of great change and creativity, crossed with Morris. Fascinating, too, is how an interest in a certain style or fashion can take root simultaneously in different people and different countries – this style had a lot of its roots in the East.

THE GREAT EXHIBITION

The International Exhibition held in Kensington, London in 1862 created enormous interest throughout Europe. For the first time Morris, Marshall & Faulkner (The Firm) exhibited their designs, inspired mainly by the art of the Middle Ages. Included were a sofa by Rossetti, a washstand by Webb and tiles designed by both of them as well as by Burne-Jones and Morris. There were stained glass, embroideries and furniture and although they were criticised by many of the traditionalists, they won two Gold Medals and enjoyed a successful launch.

Just as – if not more – significant was a Japanese section. Japan had not traded with Europe before, and the Exhibition provided the first glimpse that most visitors had ever experienced of the simple elegance of Japanese style. Its total contrast to Victorian fashion caused great excitement. At the close of the exhibition the unsold pieces were bought to form the basis of an Oriental Warehouse in the West End of London, to be managed by Arthur Lasenby Liberty, future owner of the world-famous department store in Regent Street. He became an expert in Oriental fabrics and, when he opened his own store in 1875, it became a meeting place for the cognoscenti of the time. Liberty Art Silks, soft in both texture and colour, were enthused over by many, including Morris, Rossetti and Burne-Jones. Oriental artefacts from furniture to jewellery were to be found there. This new fashion was light-years away from the neon-coloured canvaswork and heavy, stiff brocades that typified Victoriana.

When Arthur Lasenby Liberty decided to produce his own collection of fabrics, he turned to Thomas Wardle, who is better known as Morris's chief dyer. Later, both Morris and Liberty each had their own dyeing facilities on the River Wandle, taking advantage of the soft water that was particularly suitable for dyeing fabrics with madder and other natural substances. Morris was at Merton Abbey, Liberty upstream from him; William De Morgan, who had found the premises for Morris, moved close by just one year later in 1882.

C. F. A. Voysey (1875–1941) was an architect and interior designer, as well as the creator of furniture, wallpaper, textiles and metalwork. In many of the houses that he built he was responsible – like Morris – for all the details from fireplaces to windows. His greatest influences were McMurdo and Morris and his love of Japanese art was incorporated into his distinctive simple linear style. He, too, was commissioned to produce designs for Liberty.

William De Morgan met Morris in 1863 at the age of 24 and remained a lifelong friend. He abandoned his studies in Fine Arts at the Royal Academy and became a devotee of the decorative arts. Although best known for his ceramic tiles, he also produced stained glass, pottery, paintings and furniture; in later life, like Morris, he wrote books. He was a chemist as well as an artist and understood the techniques of glazing and firing so well that he was able to match exactly the Isnik tiles to complete an Islamic scheme commissioned by Lord Leighton, which can still be seen today at his magnificent house in Kensington, London. Certainly some of De Morgan's tiles have an Eastern flavour, but his work is highly individual, encompassing beauty, humour and terror (rather like the stories of Roald Dahl). Some of the animals he depicts are fascinatingly grotesque, his peacocks sumptuous, and his owls gently amusing. Other fine collections of his work are at the Debenham House in Addison Road and the Victoria & Albert Museum, both also in Kensington, London.

My lasting affection for the styles of the period was instigated by the inspiring Brangwyn Panels in Swansea, which I first saw on my seventh birthday. Frank Brangwyn

The William Morris room in the superb showrooms of Arthur Sanderson & Sons in London, showing a very small selection of their current range of Morris fabrics and wallpapers available for sale. Overseen by a portrait of Morris himself are one of the original pear-wood printing blocks, a current Sanderson hand-blocked wallpaper pattern book, 'Vine' and 'Chrysanthemum' in tapestry weave upholstery fabric, hand-blocked 'Trellis' wallpaper, and 'Marigold', both on the wall and in the foreground.

•

One of the many original Morris & Co wallpaper printing logs now owned by Arthur Sanderson & Sons and held in their design archive at Uxbridge.

was another whose life touched Morris; he was apprenticed to him in 1882. His style of painting is so distinctive that I believe that I would recognise it anywhere. Early in 1991, while on holiday on the island of Bali, my husband and I 'discovered' an octogenarian Balinese whose paintings were so like Brangwyn that it quite stunned me. Brangwyn had travelled extensively and his style, too, must surely have been influenced by that of the East.

So all the threads that tie this book together meet. I feel privileged to have been born into a country with such a rich heritage and to be able to perpetuate the work of so many great talents. Their legacy lives forever. To re-create it in our own homes is both beautiful and rewarding.

'What business have we with art at all, unless we can share it?'
WILLIAM MORRIS

COMPTON

COMPTON IS THE largest and most dramatic rug that I have ever attempted – its slow evolution was so enjoyable that I could hardly bear to finish it! But I have always been attracted to partially worked designs. The gentle movement of the background through this design is like the sea moving up and down the beach and changing the colour of the sand. I love to remember how it looked in its early stages.

The original was designed as a wallpaper and textile by Morris & Co in 1896 and destined for Compton Hall, Wolverhampton. All the hallmarks of William Morris are here; the bold flowers catch your attention but do not overpower the wonderful detail – the balance of design and background is perfect.

Arthur Sanderson & Sons of London own all of Morris & Co's original woodblocks for printing wallpaper and they still produce many designs by hand-blocking in the traditional way. Some, like Compton, have been transferred to machine to provide a more economical range of both wallpapers and fabrics. Interestingly, the design was reduced for machine and, when I enlarged it to accommodate the delicate shapes on an 8#/inch (3#/cm) rug canvas, I unknowingly returned it almost to its original proportions. As I wanted the rug to look right from every angle, I also had to give it a centre and reverse the design at either end. The original, of course, all lies in one direction – it also repeats – so the rug needed a natural ending all round. Thanks to the fine draughtsmanship of Phyllis Steed, all this has been achieved without detracting from the beauty of such a timeless classic.

My first intention was to add a decorative border, using some of the central design and adapting it, but after studying the first drawings it seemed inappropriate. The centre is so strong that an extra border would just look fussy. So I stitched a plain black border to give the effect of framing the rug and emphasising the centre.

The actual background to the central design was a problem. I felt that black was too sharp, charcoal too blue – so, in the end, charcoal, very dark green and brown were blended. This also may seem fussy, but it achieved the colour I wanted. Let's hope that you (and Morris!) approve.

The rug led naturally to the big cushion. It is worked on finer canvas, but it had to be large enough to stand up to the impact of the rug. It is just one end of the rug design –

The Compton rug, seen here nearing completion, with its companion cushion and (overleaf) – finally – in use. The two photographs help to illustrate wonderfully the true strength of this design; it blends with the elegance of a carpeted room as easily as it reflects the warmth and drama of the inglenook fireplace and stone floor.

adapted to finish neatly at the top and bottom. Some of the smaller blue flowers have been omitted as they looked unbalanced. The two together bring warmth, welcome and excitement to any room.

I know of two people who have adapted the rectangular cushion into square ones, using printed canvases and stitching just the red and pink flowers and their immediate surroundings, and adding a wide border to fit their purposes. I've not seen the results, but know that they are both pleased.

COMPTON CUSHION

CANVAS: 12# to the inch (5# to the cm)

DESIGN AREA: 15 × 21 inches (38 × 53 cm)

STITCH: Tent, with number of threads as below

NEEDLE: Size 18

YARN: Appleton Tapestry Wool (one thread)
for the design

973 – 2 skeins	205 – 1 hank
293 – 3 skeins	207 – 2 skeins
294 – 2 skeins	184 – 3 skeins
901 – 3 skeins	861 – 1 skein
762 – 2 skeins	882 – 2 skeins
984 – 2 skeins	703 – 2 skeins
986 – 1 hank	708 – 3 skeins
691 – 1 skein	155 – 1 skein
692 – 2 skeins	993 – 4 skeins
204 – 3 skeins	

Appleton Crewel Wool (four threads) for the background
588 – 2 hanks
998 – 1 hank
298 – 1 hank

These are quantities for the cushion cover shown.

The background is worked with a blend of 2 threads of 588, 1 of 998 and 1 of 298 in the needle to give the very dark, soft – but not black – hue of the original. If you find that four threads are too bulky for your tension, use just one of each of the three colours in your needle. The background may be continued for an extra two rows beyond the design. If preferred, a pure black border could be stitched; four skeins will be needed.

•

*The cushion is an adaptation of one end
of the rug; it is worked on finer canvas which creates a smaller design.
It complements the rug, of course, but stands equally well on its own –
I particularly like it on the magnificent 'Empire' bed.*

COMPTON
CUSHION

KEY

207
205
204
861
708
703
882
691
692
901
986
984
762
184
973
155
293
294
993

Background
588, 298 & 998

☆
Middle point

COMPTON MINIATURE

There is so much in the Compton design that the chart could be used for an almost endless number of projects. The charm of the red and pink flower, made tiny by being stitched on fine linen, gives me enormous pleasure. Contrasted with the strength that it has in the rug, it is easy to see that size affects us as much as colour; small things fascinate, while the same flower, greatly enlarged, will impress.

This was worked on a 28#/inch (11#/cm) linen using DMC Stranded Cotton with two strands (of the six) in a size 24 needle. Tent Stitch was used over one intersection, as I wanted to see it as small as possible; cross stitch would have made the design larger, as each stitch would need to go over two intersections. The finished size turned out as 3½ × 3½ inches (9 × 9 cm).

DMC Stranded Cotton	Appleton equivalent
3022	973
612	901
644	984
3047	692
758	204
356	205
355	207
712	882
948	703
754	708

There are the same number of stitches in this miniature picture as in the flower on which it sits. The silver frame is true Art Nouveau.

HARE & FOX

IN 1887 WILLIAM MORRIS completed the design for his tapestry 'The Forest'. It is a remarkable work, probably woven by William Knight at Merton Abbey. Originally bought by Alexander Ionides for his house at No 1 Holland Park, it is 48 inches (120 cm) high × 177 inches (450 cm) wide and is now in the collection of the Victoria & Albert Museum in London.

Morris frequently avoided drawing birds and animals in his early years of designing and more often than not recruited his friend Philip Webb, the architect, to draw them for him. The wonderful swirling forest is typically Morris and gives all the atmosphere of deep woodland. The illogicality of finding not only the Fox and Hare but also a lion, a peacock and a raven in close proximity seems to matter not at all.

The mood of the piece is medieval and the 'mille fleurs' – the flowers in the foreground – add to this. They are reminiscent of the Cluny tapestries of the sixteenth century and are believed to have been drawn partly by Philip Webb with help from Morris's most famous pupil, Henry Dearle. The knowledge that so many people could contribute to one glorious work in such a harmonious way reminds me of Morris's belief in the meaning of creative work and the joy that can be achieved through it.

To attempt to adapt the whole tapestry to one piece of needlepoint is clearly not very practical. Few rooms could accommodate such a large piece and even the most enthusiastic needleworker might find the whole project daunting. I decided therefore to start with the Hare and make it cushion size. It is an obvious choice; the Hare is shown head-on and the colours are totally naturalistic.

It worked so well that the Fox was voted an essential successor. He needed to be larger than the Hare and the foliage around him was made more lush by adding an extra shade around the veins of the leaves. I also brightened up the flowers considerably – taking into account that the original would probably have faded. The effect is that, even though the Fox is in a deeper part of the forest, a ray of sunshine has penetrated to spotlight him and the flowers. The Hare, hiding in the shadows, has seen him.

I found the two pretty chairs a few years ago and had never been able to decide on a design for them. A tracery of small flowers seemed the most suitable solution, but rather too obvious. One day, the Hare cushion was sitting on one of the chairs; it looked so completely at home that the

The Hare and the Fox cushions are taken from William Morris's 1887 tapestry 'The Forest'. Here they look perfectly at home in their natural habitat in the Surrey countryside.

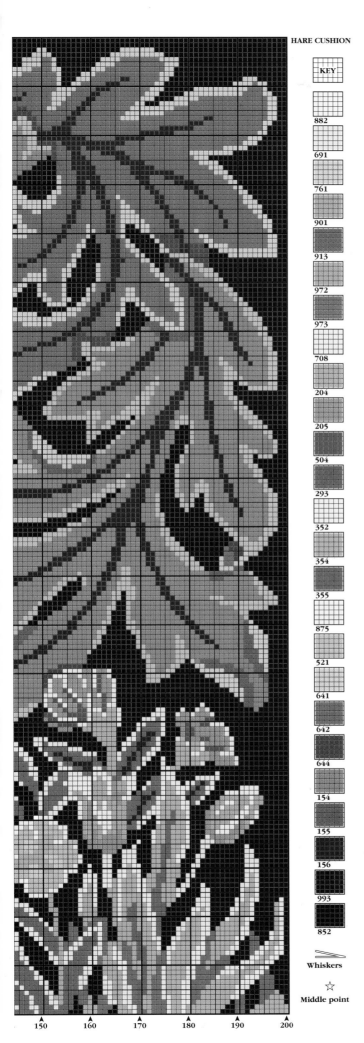

KEY

882
691
761
901
913
972
973
708
204
205
504
293
352
354
355
875
521
641
642
644
154
155
156
993
852

Whiskers

☆
Middle point

150 160 170 180 190 200

decision was taken to re-work both Hare and Fox to fit. Although the chairs are very small, the designs did not quite cover them. When the template was made, I was able to use my printed version to see how much extra was needed. The foreground had to be extended forward and to the sides – it just meant elongating the leaves and stems and making up or repeating a few on each edge. I considered extending the swirling acanthus leaves, but decided that they were too complicated. For larger chairs (and most are), you could use the chart and work on coarser canvas, though exactly how the design will need to be altered will depend on your chair. With the flowers and foliage growing in a random way, you have a great deal of freedom.

HARE CUSHION

CANVAS: 14# to the inch (5½# to the cm)

DESIGN AREA: 14 × 14 inches (36 × 36 cm)

STITCH: Tent, with 3 threads (see also page 114)

NEEDLE: Size 20

YARN: Appleton Crewel Wool

691 – 1 skein	354 – 2 skeins
901 – 1 skein	355 – 2 skeins
761 – 2 skeins	293 – 2 skeins
913 – 1 skein	852 – 1 hank (Background)
882 – 1 skein	156 – 4 skeins
972 – 3 skeins	155 – 2 skeins
973 – 1 skein	154 – 1 hank
504 – 1 skein	521 – 3 skeins
708 – 1 skein	644 – 1 skein
204 – 1 skein	642 – 1 hank
205 – 1 skein	641 – 3 skeins
875 – 1 skein	993 – 1 skein
352 – 4 skeins	

These are quantities for the cushion cover shown.

If you need to add to the design to accommodate a chair seat, or would just like to show more background, you will require more yarn – see page 113.

The original Hare contains all the colours mentioned, but, in order to move gently from one colour to another, some colours were blended together in the needle. No hares – as far as I know – are identical and the tones of their fur change as the light falls on them, so you are free to experiment with the shades and create your own unique markings. When the stitching is complete, you can give your Hare some whiskers and eyebrows, using white sewing thread to make long stitches across the surface.

25

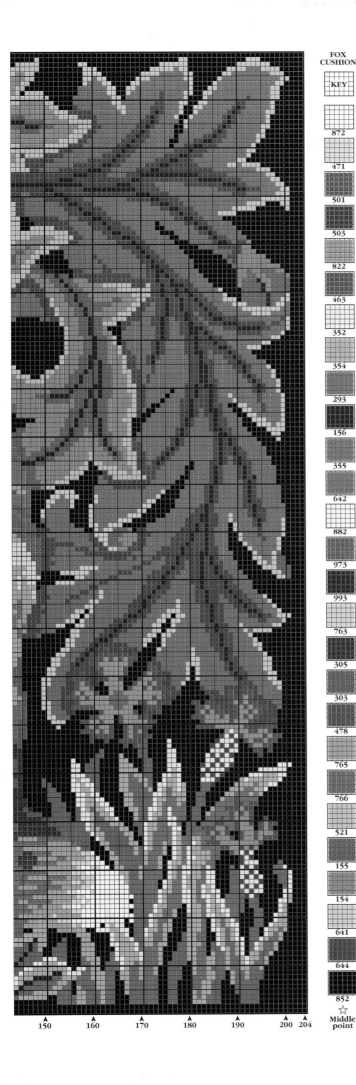

FOX
CUSHION

KEY

872
471
501
503
822
463
352
354
293
156
355
642
882
973
993
763
305
303
478
765
766
521
155
154
641
644
852
☆
Middle
point

150 160 170 180 190 200 204

FOX CUSHION

CANVAS: 14# to the inch (5½# to the cm)

DESIGN AREA: 14 × 14 inches (36 × 36cm)

STITCH: Tent, with 3 threads (see also page 114)

NEEDLE: Size 20

YARN: Appleton Crewel Wool

872 – 1 skein	993 – 1 skein
471 – 1 skein	763 – 1 skein
501 – 1 skein	305 – 1 skein
503 – 1 skein	303 – 2 skeins
822 – 1 skein	478 – 1 skein
463 – 1 skein	765 – 2 skeins
352 – 2 skeins	766 – 2 skeins
354 – 2 skeins	521 – 1 skein
293 – 2 skeins	155 – 4 skeins
156 – 2 skeins	154 – 4 skeins
355 – 2 skeins	641 – 2 skeins
642 – 1 hank	644 – 1 hank
882 – 1 skein	852 – 1 hank + 4 skeins
973 – 1 skein	(Background)

These are quantities for the cushion cover shown.

If you need to add to the design to accommodate a chair seat, or would just like to show more background, you will require more yarn – see page 113.

As in nature, the colours in foliage are quite fickle. Sometimes the veins of leaves are dark, sometimes light. As one leaf cuts the light from another, the shadow can cause two quite different shades on the same leaf – and so it is when sunlight strikes. Paint with your wools and create your own forest.

•

(Previous page)
The Hare and Fox have been adapted to fit these pretty 'spoon-back' chairs and are photographed in the beautiful library at 8 Addison Road, the house designed by Halsey Ricardo for Sir Ernest Debenham in 1904. So many details in this extraordinary house are treats for the enthusiast of fine workmanship. It is now owned by The Richmond Fellowship.

WOODPECKER

THIS WAS THE FIRST of William Morris's own designs for a tapestry. It was woven at Merton Abbey in about 1885 and the original is now at the William Morris Gallery in Walthamstow, London. As you can see, it was much longer than my version and included a honeysuckle border and a piece from a poem by Morris referring to an Italian legend where a king is turned into a woodpecker.

I once a king and chief, now am the tree bark's thief;
ever twixt trunk and leaf, chasing the prey.

The sizes of canvas available and the practicality of showing a finished piece in a modern home sometimes – regrettably – force me to adapt a design. On this occasion I have omitted the border and shortened the whole design to make it a sensible size for a firescreen. The canvas, 14 threads to the inch, afforded as much detail as was needed for this size.

The wealth of design and almost total lack of plain background reminded me once again of Frank Brangwyn; the swirling acanthus leaves almost move – in total contrast to the very still and watchful birds.

WOODPECKER

CANVAS: 14# to the inch (5½# to the cm)

DESIGN AREA: 23 × 16 inches (58 × 41 cm)

STITCH: Tent, with 3 threads (see also page 114)

NEEDLE: Size 20

YARN: Appleton Crewel Wool

352 – 1 hank	477 – 2 skeins
354 – 1 hank	474 – 4 skeins
355 – 1 hank	472 – 2 skeins
293 – 1 hank	471 – 2 skeins
294 – 4 skeins	841 – 1 skein
156 – 2 skeins	692 – 2 skeins
155 – 1 hank	913 – 1 skein
154 – 1 hank	902 – 4 skeins
521 – 1 hank	762 – 2 skeins
873 – 2 skeins	206 – 1 skein
874 – 2 skeins	993 – 1 skein
644 – 4 skeins	504 – 1 skein
642 – 1 hank	852 – 1 hank + 4 skeins
641 – 4 skeins	

These are quantities for the piece shown.

Should you wish to increase the size to fit a particular piece of furniture, but not wish to change the canvas gauge, the design could be continued in the appropriate direction. For instance, the half orange at the top right could be completed; use one of the other oranges as a colour guide. The branches could be elongated and the leaves completed. Another alternative would be to stitch a 'frame' of appropriate width in stripes of two or more colours.

•

The original Woodpecker tapestry, with
its poem, swirling acanthus leaves and honeysuckle border is a most
beautiful design. Woven in 1885, it is now in the collection of the
William Morris Gallery at Walthamstow.
My version, photographed with a miniature orange tree, is perhaps a
more practical size for the home of today.

As well as this handsome picture, the
Woodpecker would also make a marvellous firescreen. At nearly 10 feet
(3 metres), Morris's original tapestry is even longer than the
Honeysuckle bell pull. The two stitched models blend well together in a
room, as one would expect. Although bell pulls are rarely used
nowadays for their original purpose, they serve as very pretty
decorations.

321▶ 310▶ 300▶ 290▶ 280▶ 270▶ 260▶ 250▶ 240▶ 230▶ 220▶ 210▶ 200▶ 190▶ 180▶ 170▶ 160▶ 150▶

WOODPECKER

KEY

352	642	
354	641	477
355	474	
293	472	
294	471	
852	841	
156	692	
155	913	
154	902	
521	762	
873	206	
874	993	
644	504	
293 & 352	902 & 692	

☆ Middle point

35

HONEYSUCKLE

The HONEYSUCKLE BORDER to William Morris's Woodpecker tapestry is too good to be lost altogether, so here it is as a bell pull. Honeysuckle recurs frequently in Morris's designs, but I found reproducing the fineness of the petals on canvas a little daunting.

The proportions are closer to Morris's original than those of my foreshortened version of Woodpecker, though – as I have explained – the central panel would be too large for most houses (and stitchers!) if it were made to its original height. The length of Honeysuckle is, however, perfectly reasonable for a bell pull.

I am always eager to explore all the possibilities of a design. If Honeysuckle were stitched on 28#/inch (11#/cm) linen over one thread, for instance, the length should fit the depth of the shortened Woodpecker. It would measure 23 × 3 inches (58 × 7.5 cm). However, I hesitate to recommend doing this without first trying it for myself. It would be necessary to make a feature of the differences in the gauge and weight of the backing fabric, perhaps, by working Honeysuckle in stranded cottons on a dark linen. Then what could be done with the area above and below the Woodpecker? Maybe the Honeysuckle design could be adapted even more to fit across – Morris 'cheated' by covering those areas with his scroll and poem. New ideas tumble in . . . this really is where my pleasure comes from . . . the challenge . . . the involvement . . . the slight uncertainty . . . and the joy when it all goes well.

HONEYSUCKLE BELL PULL

CANVAS: 14# to the inch (5½# to the cm)

DESIGN AREA: 48½ × 6 inches (123 × 15 cm)

STITCH: Tent, with 3 threads (see also page 114)

NEEDLE: Size 20

YARN: Appleton Crewel Wool

692 – 1 hank	352 – 1 hank + 2 skeins
902 – 4 skeins	354 – 1 hank + 2 skeins
762 – 1 skein	355 – 3 skeins
913 – 2 hanks	293 – 3 skeins
703 – 2 skeins	294 – 3 skeins
708 – 2 skeins	877 – 1 skein
204 – 2 skeins	926 – 1 hank (Background)
861 – 2 skeins	

These are quantities for the bell pull shown.

The Honeysuckle bell pull welcomes us to the magnificent Stanmore Hall in Middlesex. Built between 1837 and 1850, it was purchased in 1888 by William Knox D'Arcy, who commissioned William Morris to provide the internal decoration and fittings, Edward Burne-Jones for lavish tapestries and William Lethaby to assist with stonework and general fitting-out in conjunction with Morris.

HONEYSUCKLE BELL PULL

KEY

692
913
902
762
352
354
355
293
294
877
703
708
861
204
926

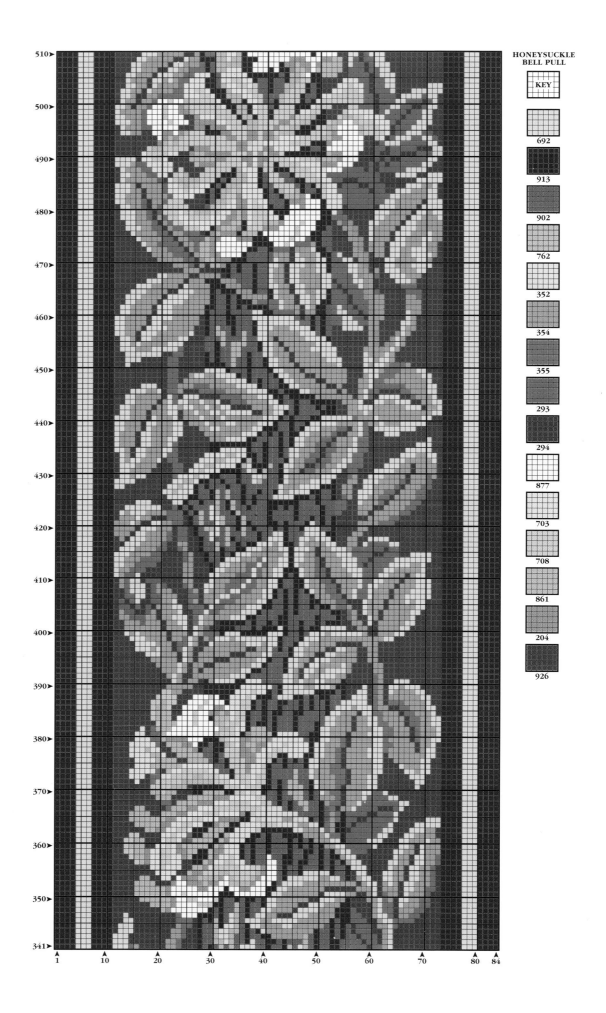

HONEYSUCKLE
BELL PULL

KEY

692

913

902

762

352

354

355

293

294

877

703

708

861

204

926

FLOWERPOT

ORRIS & CO started to produce embroidery kits in 1878. They could be bought with the outline drawn or printed on the fabric, or the design could be placed on the customer's own material. These pieces were meant as cushion covers or small panels. If desired, they could be completed by the embroideresses at Morris & Co. Although this latter activity would have brought income to Morris's firm, he preferred that the end user should be the person involved in, and enjoy the work leading up to, its realisation.

Flowerpot is one of the earliest examples of a Morris & Co kit. In her excellent book *William Morris Textiles*, Linda Parry notes that in 1875 Morris would have seen a new acquisition at the Victoria & Albert Museum: two seventeenth-century Italian designs, from which he almost certainly drew inspiration for his Flowerpot. I know of two worked samples. The one in the Victoria & Albert Museum is an embroidered piece worked in chain stitch and French knots on wool flannel. The piece that can be seen at the William Morris Gallery at Walthamstow was stitched on

*M*ay Morris's original Flowerpot
embroidery, in the collection of the William Morris Gallery.

•

*T*his 'fairy tale' cottage, which houses
more conventional flowerpots, is a perfect setting for the completed cushion.
Although Morris's Flowerpot has an Eastern feel, it blends well with
the grey of the wicker chair and the rambling twigs of the wintery
Oxfordshire countryside.

linen by his daughter, May Morris, using silks and gold thread worked in satin stitch, long and short, stem stitch and running stitch as well as chain stitch and French knots.

For me, Flowerpot has an Eastern look not apparent in similar subsequent designs for Morris kits – the Persian-style vase, the improbable symmetry of the stylised flowers and their beautiful curving stems. My version is worked on canvas using tent stitch and, of course, the whole canvas is covered, not just the outlines. The colours remain close to the original May Morris version.

The chart allows you to extract a section for a smaller project; just one flower worked on the same gauge of canvas makes a dainty pincushion.

FLOWERPOT CUSHION

CANVAS: 14# to the inch (5½# to the cm)

DESIGN AREA: 15½ × 15 inches (39 × 38 cm)

STITCH: Tent, with 3 threads (see also page 114)

NEEDLE: Size 20

YARN: Appleton Crewel Wool

873 – 1 skein	226 – 1 skein
874 – 1 hank	128 – 1 skein
353 – 4 skeins	877 – 5 skeins
354 – 4 skeins	708 – 4 skeins
355 – 4 skeins	204 – 1 skein
221 – 1 skein	761 – 3 skeins
222 – 2 skeins	762 – 5 skeins
223 – 1 skein	875 – 2 hanks
224 – 1 skein	

These are quantities for the cushion shown.

•

(Overleaf)
For many years I have admired May Morris's embroidered original, so it seems appropriate that my interpretation should be seen on a frame once used by May herself. One of her co-embroiderers at Hammersmith was Fanny Becket and it was her son-in-law, John Masterson, who kindly let me use the frame – much to my delight. The pincushion shows one of the flowers stitched on finer canvas in slightly darker coral colours.

44

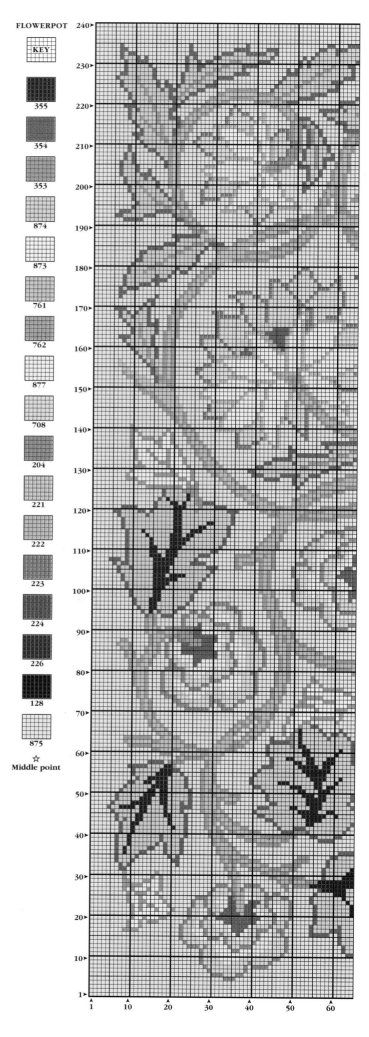

FLOWERPOT

KEY

355
354
353
874
873
761
762
877
708
204
221
222
223
224
226
128
875
☆
Middle point

JACKFIELD ROSE

A GREAT DEAL of the Ironbridge Gorge in Shropshire has been turned into a fascinating re-creation of industrial manufacturing in the 1800's. One of the most important industries in the area at that time was ceramic tile making.

In the 1860's and 1870's the influence of some of our greatest designers – William Morris, William De Morgan, Edward Burne-Jones and Walter Crane – caused a similar revolution in tile design to those which they were creating in textile design, painting and illustration. The Jackfield Tile Museum has a superb display of many of the better tiles from this period. My visit there was all too short, but my memory of a washstand with a tiled back was most vivid. It featured a group of tiles, each showing a different flower which spills over its borders. There was such a lot of design in so small an area that I wanted to see them individually, so that they could not detract from each other. Here is the Rose, with its lovely geometric border.

I have adapted it slightly – there are only two roses on the small tile but the larger format left rather a lot of background to stitch, so another flower has been added. The background was originally a very deep blue, which you might like to try. I see the 'tile' not just as a cushion or picture but possibly two of them inset on the front of a chest or pretty door – or as a workbox or table top.

You can see that just part of the design can also be used to decorate a tablecloth and the theme could be continued by stitching a single rosebud onto each napkin. A tray cloth might have a small sprig of a rose, a twig and a few leaves – with the chart you are free to choose how little or how much you wish to show.

My inspiration for this embroidery came from the beautiful tiles on this Victorian washstand at the Jackfield Tile Museum in Ironbridge. As you can see, there are many others here to inspire!
My first version was intended as a picture and has been mounted on a board ready for framing.

•

A part of the design has been transferred to the corner of a tablecloth. The photograph below shows how we marked its position with tacking stitches.
(Overleaf) The design on the white linen tablecloth contrasts interestingly with the heavier wool version, now made into a cushion.

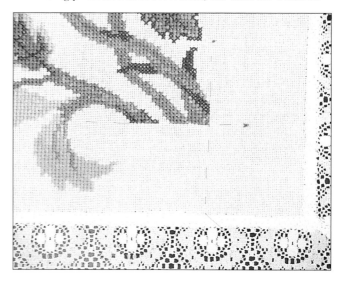

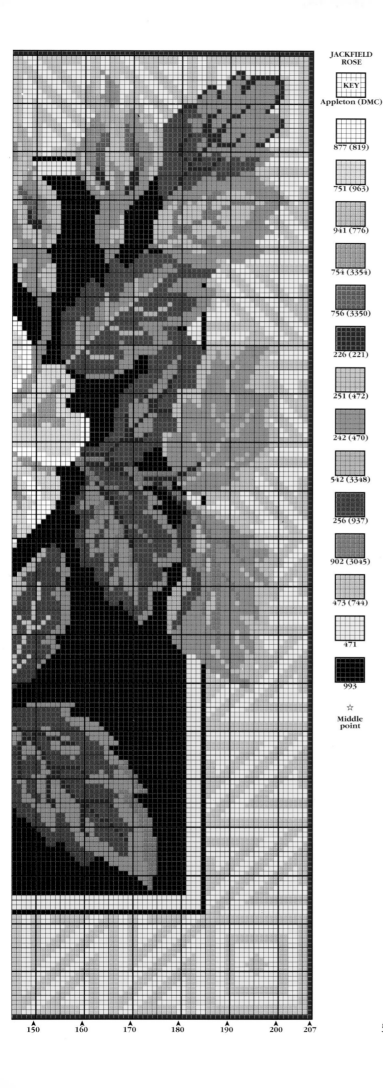

877 (819)

751 (963)

941 (776)

754 (3354)

756 (3350)

226 (221)

251 (472)

242 (470)

542 (3348)

256 (937)

902 (3045)

473 (744)

471

993

☆
Middle
point

JACKFIELD ROSE

CUSHION/PICTURE

CANVAS: 14# to the inch (5½# to the cm)

DESIGN AREA: 14½ × 14½ inches (37 × 37 cm)

STITCH: Tent, with 3 threads (see also page 114)

NEEDLE: Size 20

YARN: Appleton Crewel Wool

877 – 2 skeins	242 – 5 skeins
751 – 4 skeins	542 – 1 skein
941 – 2 skeins	256 – 4 skeins
754 – 4 skeins	902 – 2 skeins
756 – 1 skein	471 – 1 hank
226 – 2 skeins	473 – 1 hank
251 – 2 skeins	993 – 1 hank

These are quantities for the cushion cover/picture shown.

TABLECLOTH

LINEN: 28# to the inch (11# to the cm)

DESIGN AREA: 9½ × 9½ inches (24 × 24 cm)

STITCH: Cross, with 2 threads of the six-stranded Cotton

NEEDLE: Size 24

YARN: DMC Stranded Cotton (in brackets on chart)

819 – 1 skein	472 – 1 skein
963 – 2 skeins	470 – 1 skein
776 – 1 skein	3348 – 1 skein
3354 – 1 skein	937 – 1 skein
3350 – 1 skein	3045 – 1 skein
221 – 1 skein	744 – 1 skein

These are quantities for the tablecloth shown.

As the Cross Stitch on the 28# linen tablecloth is worked over two threads, the design remains exactly the same size as on the 14# canvas. It was an ideal choice for the corner of a cloth as the stem emerges from the corner of the picture. The effect would have been crowded if it had touched the lace so 51 linen threads were counted out and marked with a tacking thread to form the 'inside corner'; the tacking is, of course, removed after the design is finished. I have to confess that, to make life easy, I bought the tablecloth complete, including the lace. It measures 54 inches (137 cm) square. For a smaller cloth I would advise using a smaller part of the design, or working this larger part over one thread only (Tent Stitch would be safer – see page 118).

AFRICAN MARIGOLD

THE WILLIAM MORRIS Gallery in Walthamstow houses, amongst other lovely things, the original watercolour for this Morris design. I was immediately attracted by its unfinished 'working drawing' quality and by the extremely delicate blues. Unlike Pomegranate (page 66), African Marigold did achieve maturity and is still being produced by Liberty of London as a curtain and furnishing fabric. The colours in the Liberty versions are necessarily more simplistic than the watercolour, but they make several interesting alternative colour combinations, showing very clearly how different a design can look when colours are changed. However, the sweeping, swirling movement of the leaves is, whatever the colouring, unmistakably Morris.

There are two parts to this design; I have chosen the large main flower as the centre of my adaptation. The blue leaves that ribbon around the large flower required very careful shading to keep the blue true to the original and retain the movement and depth. The large flower, with its very soft colouring, was no easier – one can shade subtly from white to blue or light yellow with watercolours, but producing the same delicacy in solid wools and pre-ordained stitch shapes is quite a challenge and several

'roughs' were stitched for this design. In the Liberty version, the Marigolds are shown in a light orange, but I preferred to retain the faded look of the original watercolour.

It would be most enjoyable – and another challenge – to make a partner with one of the smaller flowers as the focal point. The complete design would also make a lovely rug and I have promised myself to undertake that one day, increasing the gauge of the canvas and producing a series of squares which could be stitched together and surrounded with an attractive border. Or, working on much finer canvas, one of the smaller marigolds would make a very pretty pincushion or potpourri sachet.

The delicate watercolour shows Morris's first interpretation of the design and the one I fell in love with; it can be seen at the William Morris Gallery, Walthamstow. 'Tom Tit', the cat, seems more interested in African Marigolds than snowdrops! (Overleaf) The colours of the cushion blend perfectly with the soft pine and a marvellous collection of blue and white transferware china.

AFRICAN MARIGOLD

CANVAS: 12# to the inch (5# to the cm)

DESIGN AREA: 15½ × 15½ inches (39 × 39 cm)

STITCH: Tent, with 1 thread

NEEDLE: Size 18

YARN: Appleton Tapestry Wool

691 – 2 skeins	321 – 1 hank
692 – 1 skein	322 – 1 skein
693 – 1 skein	324 – 3 skeins
901 – 1 skein	325 – 2 skeins
876 – 2 skeins	352 – 4 skeins
521 – 4 skeins	293 – 2 skeins
641 – 2 skeins	992 – 1 hank + 3 skeins

These are quantities for the cushion cover shown.

If you need to add to the design, or would just like to show more background, you will require more yarn – see page 113.

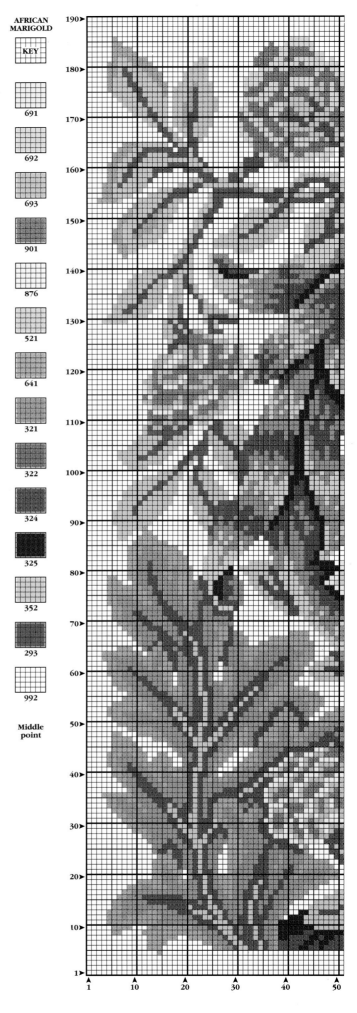

JASMINE

JASMINE TRAIL was one of Morris's earliest known fabric designs; its light, delicate and meandering stems, flowers and leaves make it a perfect subject for a repeating pattern. Here is just a section, with no repeats; the plant shapes allow me the freedom to stop and leave a space for an initial without appearing unnatural.

My original interpretation fitted the top of a small workbox for which no background stitching was necessary, as the pale yellow of the fine canvas provided a suitable tone. Naturally, great care had to be taken to avoid carrying the threads across a blank area at the back of the work.

It was worked again as a tiny cushion, which could also double as a container for sweet-smelling herbs (or something scented with jasmine).

I tried it a third time with pink-edged flowers instead of the original colourway. In this version (from the same chart) the flowers and leaves are stitched in stranded cottons to give them a sheen. The trellis is worked in wool, using a line of back stitch on either side of the tent stitch to imitate the grain of the wood. The border of this version is the invention of Angela Kahan; it gives a lovely lacy effect. The centre of the diamonds are over eight canvas threads, reducing down to two. The corners are mitred.

Increasing the size of this design by working on a coarser gauge of canvas did not appeal to me as I like the delicacy of the flowers. There are numerous ways to increase the size of a cushion; the worked piece can be attached to a ready-made larger cushion, or you could add a frill or a lace edging. It really depends on which version has been stitched, where it is intended to rest and your personal preference.

JASMINE

CANVAS: 17# to the inch (7# to the cm)

DESIGN AREA: 8½ × 8½ inches (22 × 22 cm)
9½ × 9½ inches (24 × 24 cm) with border

NEEDLE: Size 22

YELLOW FLOWER VERSION (1st colourway)

STITCH: Tent, with two threads

YARN: Appleton Crewel Wool

991b – 1 skein	547	– 2 skeins
844 – 1 skein	901	– 1 skein
551 – 1 skein	765	– 1 skein
255 – 2 skeins		
Cushion background: 882 – 1 hank		

PINK FLOWER VERSION (2nd colourway)

STITCH: Tent and Backstitch, with one thread (six strands) of Cotton or two threads of Wool

YARN: DMC Stranded Cotton

Blanc – 1 skein	581	– 3 skeins
963 – 1 skein	937	– 3 skeins
819 – 1 skein		

761 – 1 skein (Appleton Crewel Wool)
764 – 1 skein (Appleton Crewel Wool)
Background: 875 – 1 hank (Appleton Crewel Wool)

To position your chosen initial, find the centre of the relevant space on the canvas (after completing the design and before stitching the background) and mark with a knot. On the charts, the optical centre of each initial is marked ☆. Count from there, using the two shades of Appleton green (255 and 547) or DMC (581 and 937).

If the background is not going to be stitched, it is essential that the threads are not run across unworked parts of the canvas as they will show through. Note that both of the yellow flower versions are worked entirely in Tent Stitch. For the pink flower version, the trellis has been stitched with a central row of Tent Stitch and the two outside rows in Backstitch (*see below*). This arrangement takes up less space than the three rows of Tent Stitch on the chart. You will need to adjust the leaves where they pass under the trellis – a few extra stitches may be needed to make this convincing. The border can be stitched all in Tent Stitch if you wish.

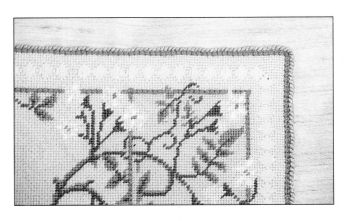

(Opposite)
My latest version of Jasmine – the plant shows how accurate Morris's drawing is. On pages 64/65, the first Jasmine as a box lid and as a tiny cushion. It seems appropriate that they are all shown in sunshine.

JASMINE

	KEY	255 (581)	551 (819)	901	991B (Blanc)	547 (937)	844 (963)	765	882	☆
Appletons 1st colourway (DMC) (Appletons 2nd colourway)				(761)				(764)	(875)	**Middle point**

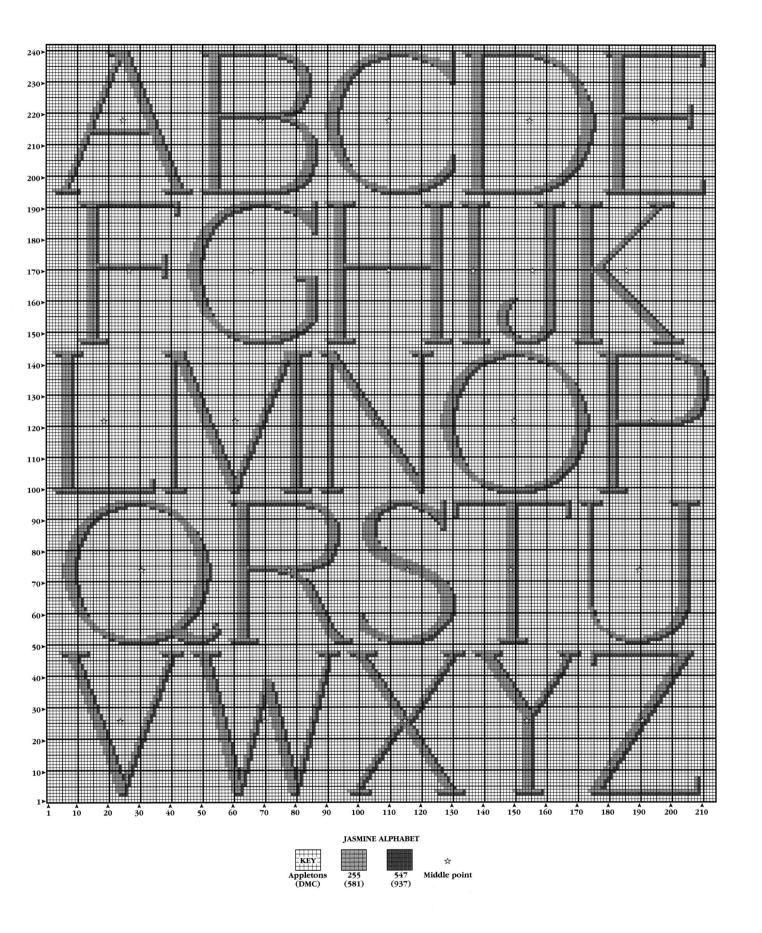

JASMINE ALPHABET

KEY			
Appletons (DMC)	255 (581)	547 (937)	☆ Middle point

POMEGRANATE

THIS RUG is based on an unfinished pencil, ink and watercolour painting attributed to Morris some time between 1880–1896 and never, to my knowledge, previously completed as a worked piece. The original painting is in the collection of the Victoria & Albert Museum.

As always, I was first attracted by the 'unfinished' look of the Morris painting and willingly took up the challenge of completing it. Whilst retaining his original colours, I hope that at the same time I have also achieved (humbly!)

something that perhaps even William Morris himself never did! Fortunately, the perfect symmetry of the design made completion comparatively simple without any alteration – and with no doubt that one was doing justice to the artist.

Particularly attractive – and unusual – is the variety of background colours. The lovely curves, so typical of this period, are used as a means to separate the different areas. The intricate central area is also perfectly complemented by the gentle simplicity of the border.

At the beginning I was a little disturbed by the fruit shapes being dark brown – not an attractive colour for fruit, especially as they resemble pineapples and strawberries. However, it was felt that any changes would perhaps lose Morris's creative vision and destroy the balance of the design.

Morris does not seem to have given a name to this piece of work, so I invented one. 'Pineapples' and 'Strawberries' were discounted and, since the centre of the design re-

(Far left) M*orris's original unfinished watercolour which inspired my rug.*

(Above) T*his fabulous mosaic covers the floor of the main reception room in Stanmore Hall. It was exciting to see it for the first time – no-one had told me of its existence. The room is very large, hence the proportionately large design. The leaves, shapes and flowing stems are so typically Morris that just placing Pomegranate on the stones was sufficient – the photograph was complete.*

minded me of pomegranate seeds, it became 'Pomegranate'. Although there are other Morris designs with this title, it still seems the most appropriate name.

Although the shapes are relatively simple, this is the most difficult of all the designs to adapt by using the chart in a different way. A new colour scheme would take a considerable time to work out; the background to each section would need to be stitched as well as the foreground shapes. It also proved difficult to extract a part of the design; the centre does not work very well as a cushion. The whole central panel, however, would work as a piano stool top stitched on finer canvas; you would need to calculate carefully and increase the border if necessary.

POMEGRANATE RUG

CANVAS: 8# to the inch (3# to the cm)

DESIGN AREA: 25 × 50 inches (64 × 127 cm)

STITCH: Cross, with 1 thread (see also page 114)

NEEDLE: Size 16

YARN: Appleton Tapestry Wool

764 – 5 hanks	542 – 4 hanks
761 – 3 skeins	873 – 1 hank
588 – 5 hanks + 3 skeins	882 – 3 skeins
185 – 1 skein	128 – 2 skeins
184 – 3 skeins	125 – 2 skeins
201 – 2 skeins	202 – 2 skeins
153 – 2 hanks + 3 skeins	297 – 1 hank
521 – 2 hanks	692 – 1 hank + 3 skeins
875 – 1 hank + 3 skeins	355 – 3 skeins
356 – 2 hanks	325 – 2 hanks

These are quantities for the rug shown.

If you would like to fringe the rug, you will need to buy cord (or you can use wool) – see page 122.

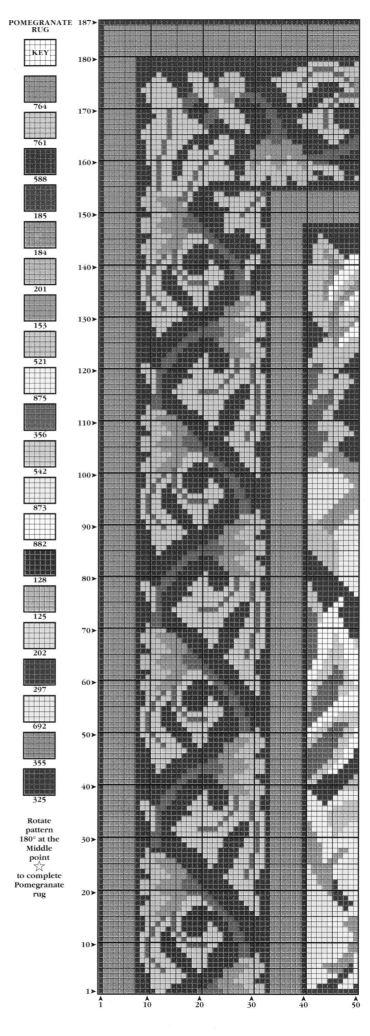

POMEGRANATE RUG

KEY

764
761
588
185
184
201
153
521
875
356
542
873
882
128
125
202
297
692
355
325

Rotate pattern 180° at the Middle point ☆ to complete Pomegranate rug

MORRIS

SOME YEARS AGO I was allowed to trace this outline, attributed to Morris. There was no name for it and no colourings.

The idea of a square rug made from such a strong and elegant design appealed to me. I spent much time stitching different colourways and finally settled on brown for the background as it was a colour not used much in my Designers Forum range and we felt it might harmonise with the decor of a wider range of homes.

Since then I have hankered after some of the other colour schemes that were considered at the time. Preparing this book seemed an ideal excuse to try out some other colours and also provided a practical lesson to illustrate the use of charts. The rug is on 8#/inch (3#/cm) canvas and measures 42 inches (107 cm) square. The cushions are on 18#/inch (7#/cm) canvas and will measure 18½ inches (46 cm) square. The number of rows on the outside edge have been reduced.

The two partially worked cushions are an opportunity to see the effect that colours have on each other. The shapes in the charts have been adhered to strictly; sometimes the arrangement, as well as the choice, of the colours has been altered. Very often changing colours alters the balance and there is a need for more (or less) weight in a certain part of the design. I feel sure you will be surprised to learn that three out of the four pinks are the same in each cushion and that the darkest of the greens – the fronds in the corner of the centre panels – is exactly the same in each. The dark blue version has had the yellows softened from those used in the brown rug.

The background in the centre of the light grey cushion has, however, reduced the palest of the green fronds to a soft impression of a design and the tips of the light blue 'petals' are rather lost. If the backgrounds were reversed, the mid green could be used in the border (as in the brown version) but the very palest pink in the centre would need to be strengthened.

Given time and patience, using charts is fascinating. If you remove the worry of whether or not the design works as a shape, all your concentration can be directed at experimenting with colours.

•

On the landing at Stanmore Hall. The shape of the ceiling is repeated in the window and in the balustrade, and slightly echoed in the rug. Stanmore Hall was one of the largest commissions for Morris & Co and the most significant before William Morris's death. Sadly, a fire destroyed some of the interior, but much of the stone and wood work has been painstakingly replaced and returned to its former glory. The Burne-Jones tapestries survived and are now in a private collection.

MORRIS

RUG

CANVAS: 8# to the inch (3# to the cm)

DESIGN AREA: 42 × 42 inches (107 × 107 cm)

STITCH: Cross, with 1 thread (see also page 114)

NEEDLE: Size 16

YARN: Appleton Tapestry Wool

842 – 2 hanks + 3 skeins	293 – 3 hanks + 3 skeins
872 – 1 hank	877 – 1 hank
762 – 2 hanks + 3 skeins	202 – 2 hanks
251 – 5 hanks + 3 skeins	204 – 2 hanks
242 – 5 hanks + 3 skeins	207 – 1 hank
128 – 5 hanks + 3 skeins (Background to border)	
585 – 12 hanks (Background to central panel)	

These are the quantities for the rug shown.

CUSHIONS

CANVAS: 18# to the inch (7# to the cm)

DESIGN AREA: 18¼ × 18¼ inches (46 × 46 cm)

STITCH: Tent, with 2 threads

NEEDLE: Size 22

YARN: Appleton Crewel Wool (in the same order as rug list above)

BLUE CUSHION:	GREY CUSHION:	
692	154	4 skeins
841	521	2 skeins
128	964	4 skeins
351	352	1 hank + 2 skeins
342	354	4 skeins
293	293	6 skeins
704	181	2 skeins
202	202	4 skeins
204	204	4 skeins
124	124	2 skeins
929	989	1 hank + 2 skeins
326	151	2 hanks + 2 skeins

These are the quantities for the COMPLETE cushions.

•

Partially stitched cushions, using the Morris rug design and changing the gauge of canvas and some of the colours. They provide a fascinating example of how the background colour can affect the design colours; the pinks in the border and green in the fronds are the same in each cushion.

Although they appear to be identical, the 'squares' of the canvas vary fractionally in either direction – ie the distance covered by, say, 200 stitches across the width is marginally different to that covered by 200 stitches along its length. This is simply caused by the method of production. I also had to make small changes to the exact symmetry of the original drawing to make it 'fit'. Caution is therefore required when following the chart to ensure that you make allowances for these discrepancies. The corner of the chart shown can be copied exactly for its DIAGONALLY OPPOSITE corner, but the ADJACENT corners are 'mirror' images of each other according to which direction you are working.

Rotate pattern 180° at middle point to complete Morris Rug.

160 170 180 190 200 210 220 230 240 250 260 270 280 290 300 311

MORRIS RUG

KEY	842	872	762	251	242	293

877	202	204	207	128	585	☆ Middle point

75

KAZAK

WILLIAM MORRIS was a collector of Eastern rugs – he used them for wall hangings, not for the floor. His connection with the designs of the East has been discussed at the beginning of this book; it seemed natural to include an example.

This design would have been contemporary with Morris and his colleagues. The name Kazak means that it originated from the Caucasus and the original might well have been worked by nomadic tribesmen as they travelled on horseback between the Caspian Sea and the Black Sea. Many of the Kazak shapes represented insects such as tarantulas; the nomads included these in order to conquer their fear of them. The zig-zag border is also typical of such rugs. The design has none of the flowing shapes we associate with Morris; it has instead the angular look that featured a little later in the Art Deco period. It is, however, an excellently balanced and well-proportioned rug that I feel would have been admired by contemporary designers and it fits comfortably with the European designs of the late nineteenth and early twentieth centuries. As with most Eastern rugs, the original from which my Kazak was taken was not quite symmetrical. Muslim beliefs dictate that 'only Allah is perfect' and deliberate mistakes are woven in, but I have straightened out all the differences to reduce confusion.

Although the bold colours contrast with most of the others in this book, they were all made from natural dyestuffs (such as madder for the warm reds) which, of course, is what Morris himself advocated.

To illustrate the versatility of charts, we also made a bag – a carpet bag, in fact. The rug border is omitted, the gauge of canvas reduced and the arrangement of the central design adjusted so that the flap of the bag echoes the design beneath it. One of my customers, who wanted something more capacious, stitched a bag using canvas the same gauge as the rug. I had brightened the bag colours a little, but she kept to those of the rug, thus retaining more of a true carpet-bag look.

•

This really dramatic setting is perfect for the Kazak Rug. It is seen here at 8 Addison Road, London, in the entrance hall with its wonderful gallery on three sides. The mosaic depicts members of the Debenham family and was executed by two Italian brothers. The deep blue tiles and decorated frieze behind are all by De Morgan. The outside of this imposing house is tiled in blue at the top to reflect the sky and green at the bottom to echo the trees.

KAZAK RUG

KEY

323

695

297

882

691

998

209

☆
Middle point

207 200 190 180 170 160 150 140 130 120

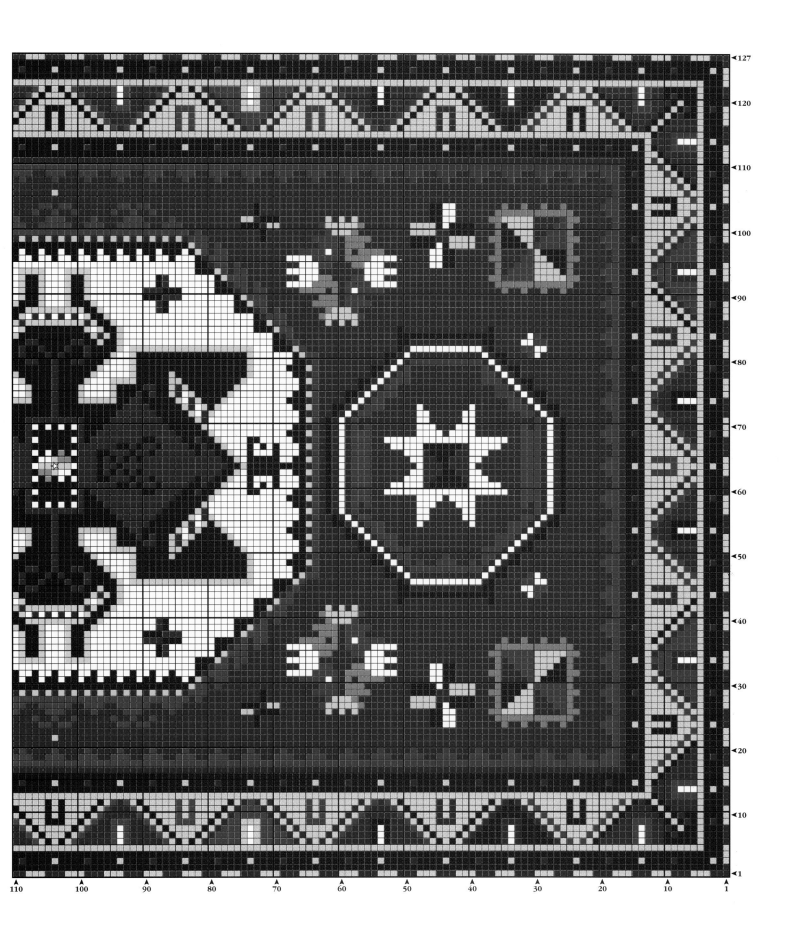

KAZAK RUG

CANVAS: 6# to the inch (2½# to the cm)

DESIGN AREA: 21 × 34 inches (53 × 86 cm)

STITCH: Cross, with 2 threads

NEEDLE: Size 16

YARN: Appleton Tapestry Wool

323 − 3 skeins
695 − 1 hank
297 − 3 hanks
882 − 3 hanks
691 − 3 hanks
998 − 6 hanks
209 − 9 hanks

These are quantities for the rug shown.

If you would like to fringe the rug, you will need to buy cord (or you can use wool) − see page 122.

KAZAK BAG & STRAP

CANVAS: 8# to the inch (3# to the cm)

DESIGN AREA: 13 × 26 inches (33 × 66 cm)

The bag has two sides of 10½ × 13 inches (27 × 33 cm) with a flap of 5 inches (13 cm).

CANVAS REQUIRED: 17 × 30 inches (43 × 76 cm) plus 3 × 48 inches (8 × 122 cm) for the strap

STITCH: Cross, with 1 thread (see also page 114)

NEEDLE: Size 16

YARN: Appleton Tapestry Wool

929 − 1 hank + 3 skeins
297 − 1 hank
564 − 3 skeins
882 − 1 hank + 3 skeins
474 − 3 skeins
504 − 4 hanks

These are quantities for the bag shown, including the strap.

For the strap you can use whatever colour yarns you have left after stitching the main part of the bag or you can follow the chart.

STRAP: Starting with the central stripe, stitch a total of 7 stripes along the whole length − leave ½ inch (1 cm) unworked at each end to stitch into the base of the bag. As the centre of the strap which goes over your shoulder looks best if it is stitched on both sides, you need to increase the number of stripes in the middle of the strap by 3 on each side; count up 74 stitches from each end (these sections form the gusset along each edge of the bag when it is made up) and then increase the width as described to 13 stripes − the 14th is the one which stitches the two edges of the central piece together (see below).

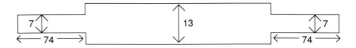

ASSEMBLY: The base of the bag is formed by the 5 rows of red background between the two smaller octagons and the blue edge of the octagons − 7 stitches in all.

Stitch the end of the strap to the outer edge of the bag exactly level with these 7 stitches, using strong thread and backstitch − matching stitch for stitch. Then, matching the edges of the strap to the edges of the bag, continue stitching up the side of the bag for 74 stitches (the point at which the strap gets wider). To join the strap together in the middle, fold so that the raw edges overlap. Your final row of Cross Stitches must be made to go through two layers of canvas to create a perfect join.

A cotton lining can give your bag that little extra professional touch, including a pocket if desired. Make sure that at least one row of cross stitch is folded under at the front of the bag so that the lining is invisible on that edge when the bag is closed. You could also add a fastening such as the magnetic ones that you find on many handbags.

•

The bag was adapted from the Kazak rug.
The colours are slightly brighter and the canvas gauge finer, making the proportions smaller. You can see how the strap forms the gusset. Shown here in a sporting atmosphere, the bag can be equally at home in more elegant surroundings.

**KAZAK BAG
& STRAP**

KEY

504

929

882

297

474

564

☆
Middle point

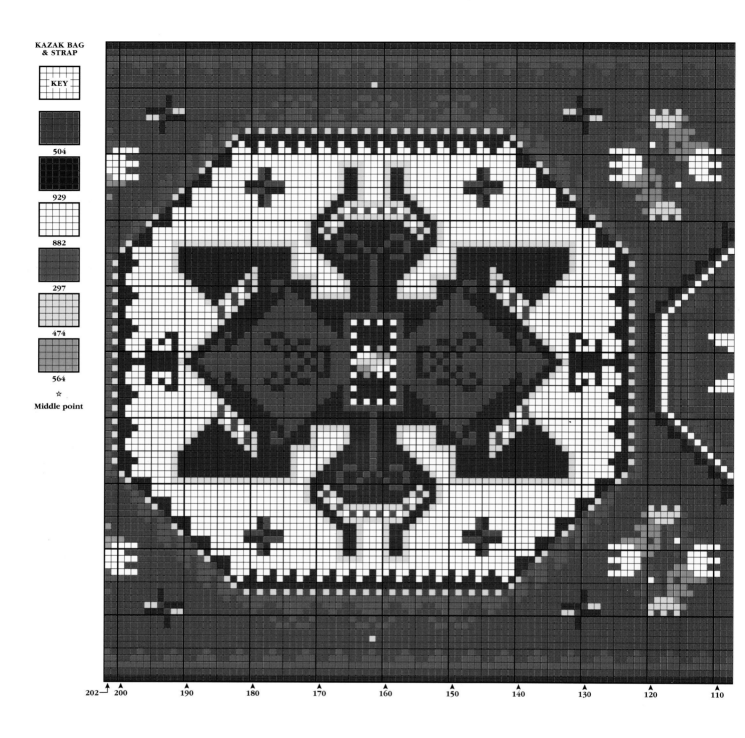

202 → 200   190   180   170   160   150   140   130   120   110

┌─ Repeat the design to this point to complete strap.

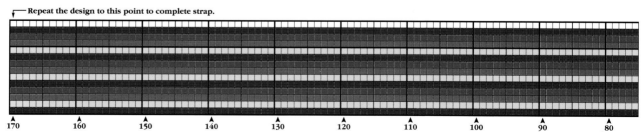

170   160   150   140   130   120   110   100   90   80

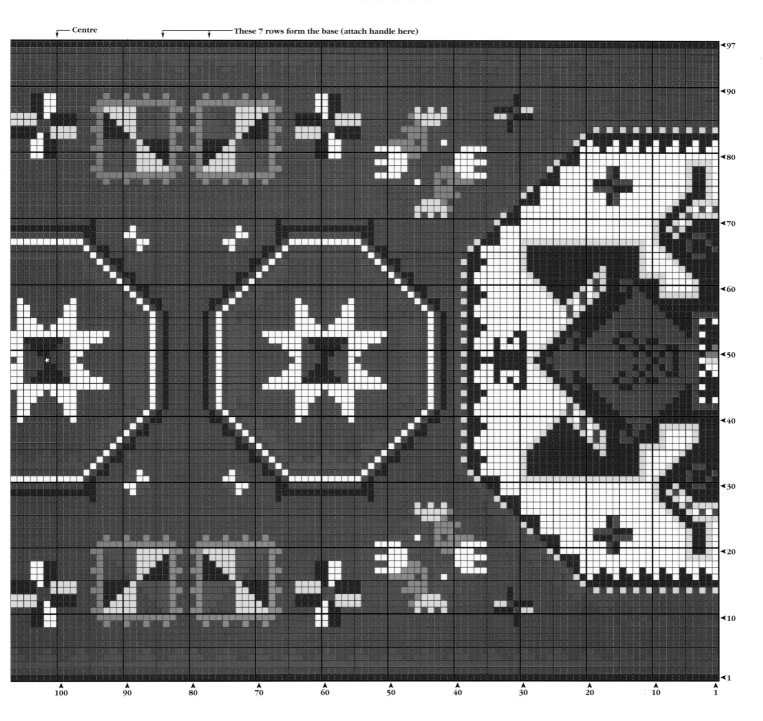

Centre — These 7 rows form the base (attach handle here)

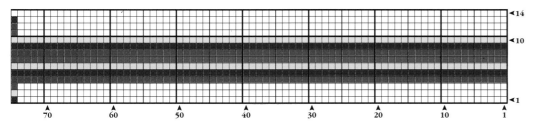

ANEMONES

ALTHOUGH MY TASTES usually run to more muted colours, anemones are one of my favourite flowers; I also like designs where the flowers or foliage overlap a border – in a similar way to the Jackfield Rose (page 48). When I saw a photograph of a beautiful Art Nouveau box lid from the early part of this century, I had found the perfect combination. The wonderful array of colourful anemones had been painted by Lucia Mathews for the Furniture Shop, which she ran with her designer husband in San Francisco from 1906–1920.

I love the uninhibited air that anemones have, mixing mauves, fuchsias and reds with such abandon. Every year I plant a few and although each individual flower has a power and strength of its own, the naivety of their vibrant colours is most evident when there are masses of blooms.

As you can see, there are several ways that you can use the chart – a cushion, a footstool and a wonderfully delicate miniature (my favourite). A single flower could also be extracted and stitched on table napkins . . . a row of them, still slightly overlapping, can be cross-stitched around a linen tablecloth . . . a rectangular stool top can be worked by stitching the design twice on canvas, side by side, and filling in the gaps at the top and bottom with some of the other flowers. Use the overlapping nature of the design to your advantage and, as long as you choose the individual flowers carefully, it should all look perfectly natural.

ANEMONES

CANVAS: 12# to the inch (5# to the cm)

DESIGN AREA: 10½ × 10½ inches (27 × 27 cm)

STITCH: Tent, with 1 thread

NEEDLE: Size 18

YARN: Appleton Tapestry Wool

447	– 3 skeins	991b	– 3 skeins
504	– 2 skeins	875	– 2 skeins
801	– 3 skeins	821	– 3 skeins
803	– 2 skeins	824	– 2 skeins
454	– 2 skeins	993	– 2 skeins
456	– 1 skein	296	– 4 hanks
			(1 hank for footstool)

LINEN: 28# to the inch (11# to the cm)

DESIGN AREA: 4 × 4 inches (10 × 10 cm)

STITCH: Tent, with two strands (from the six in the thread) over one intersection

NEEDLE: Size 24

YARN: DMC Stranded Cotton (shown in brackets on chart key)

666	– 1 skein	Blanc	– 1 skein
498	– 1 skein	3072	– 1 skein
3608	– 1 skein	798	– 1 skein
3607	– 1 skein	796	– 1 skein
553	– 1 skein	310	– 1 skein
550	– 1 skein		

Mark out the background before stitching. The stool in the photograph is 10 inches (25 cm) in diameter. You will need to mark a circle – a 'compass' can be made by putting the canvas on a board, tacking some string to the centre point of the canvas, tying a pencil to the other end the required distance away (half the proposed diameter) and drawing a circle. Or you can place an appropriately sized plate on the canvas as close to the centre as possible and trace a line around it. Find the centre of the circle by folding the canvas in half twice.

•

*The miniature version, looking so delicate,
is stitched on linen in stranded cottons, showing the whole design.
Overleaf, the cushion, footstool and miniature are all shown together – the
vibrant colours light up the whole picture wonderfully. I do admire these
flowers, with their joie de vivre.*

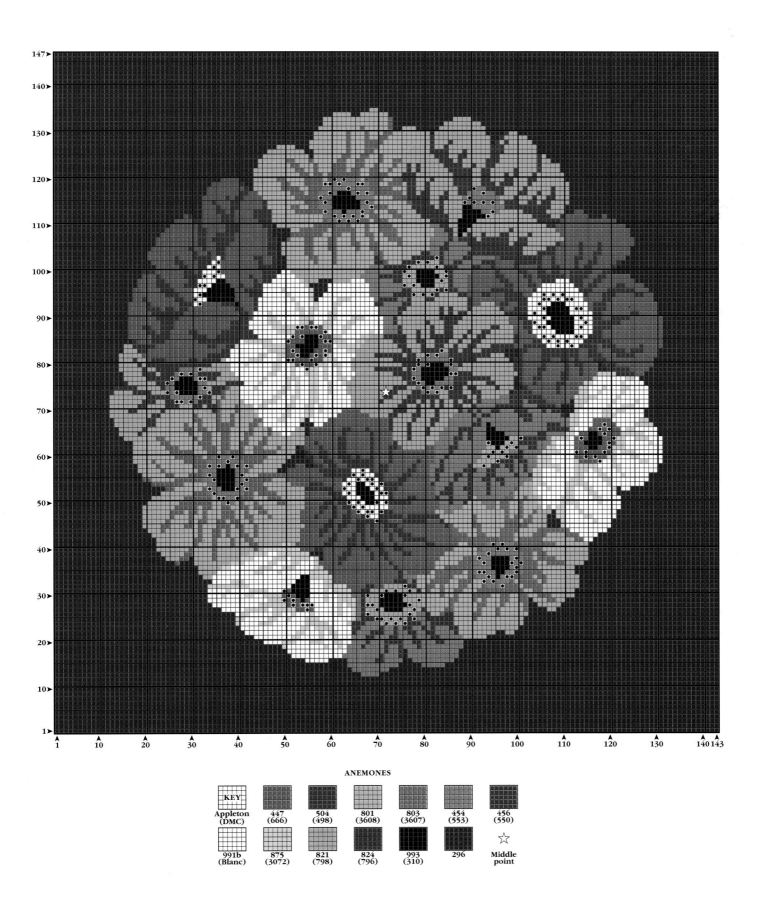

ANEMONES

KEY

Appleton (DMC)	447 (666)	504 (498)	801 (3608)	803 (3607)	454 (553)	456 (550)
991b (Blanc)	875 (3072)	821 (798)	824 (796)	993 (310)	296	Middle point

OWLS &
RABBITS

THESE MAKE ME smile every time I see them. The designs both belong to William De Morgan and were originally 6-inch tiles made close to Morris's workshop at Merton Abbey. I've not been able to decide if the owls are drunk or just tired – or if the original was supposed to be a 'stop-frame' of one owl in his demise. The colourings are mine and, in the cause of continuity, I added a branch or two.

The original Rabbits remind me of my childhood and they shouldn't really be running around a branch. I'm afraid that De Morgan's originals, although definitely rabbits (I can tell by their ears) have rather odd bodies and lambs' tails – but, with a little help from Julie Russell and Phyllis Steed, they are now young rabbits.

It seemed a shame not to use these designs in another way. To see them as individual owls or rabbits – on fine linen or canvas, a little owl or rabbit badge would be quite charming. Either could be worked on a pillowcase or blouse using waste canvas (see page 113). They could become a little 'trademark' for a child; sufficient designs have been shown as miniatures in this book to enable you to imagine this.

The idea of a child's rug came to mind. Perhaps a series of squares? Perhaps another design in the same vein, so that three squares could be repeated twice? This third design did not happen in time, although I have several in mind. The problem of how to position the Owls and Rabbits so that they lie in a logical way proved difficult; it was Angela Kahan who suggested mirror-imaging the Rabbits. It makes the rug suitable for the side of a child's bed and the child can decide which way the rabbits should be facing, the bed or the room. It also makes a lovely wall-hanging . . . a throw for a toy box . . . or a double-width headboard. The rabbits are the same colour, but the background was changed to look less sophisticated and more suitable for a child's room. You'll notice that the design overlaps the border unevenly (my husband's idea – I said earlier that it's a real family affair!); this is to shorten the rug and improve the proportions. The border could also contain daisies or carrots or

·

The Owls and Rabbits cushions tucked into the overmantel of a large, but dramatically simple, stone fireplace in Stanmore Hall. We considered photographing the Owls at night on one of the turrets of the lovely Hall, but decided it was rather less practical.

whatever you feel appropriate. Should you use a border around the cushions, it will need to be even all around to make each a square.

Originally, the backgrounds for the cushions were worked (in Gobelin Filling stitch) in two shades of blue to depict the darkening sky but, as often happens, colours that looked sufficiently different in the hand looked almost the same when stitched. My fault was in not working enough on my 'rough' to see how it looked in reality. If you like the idea of this effect, I suggest that you spend a little time experimenting.

The humour of both the Owls and the Rabbits has given me enormous pleasure both in the making and the finished results.

OWLS CUSHION

CANVAS: 12# to the inch (5# to the cm)

DESIGN AREA: 13 × 13 inches (33 × 33 cm)

STITCH: (Design) Tent, with 1 thread (Background) Gobelin Filling or Tent

NEEDLE: Size 18

YARN: Appleton Tapestry Wool (Crewel or Tapestry for background)

974 – 2 skeins	882 – 3 skeins
911 – 3 skeins	991 – 1 skein
913 – 3 skeins	993 – 1 skein
304 – 1 skein	842 – 1 skein
761 – 3 skeins	242 – 2 skeins
764 – 2 skeins	335 – 2 skeins

Background:
926 – 3 hanks (Tapestry or Crewel)

These are quantities for the cushion cover shown.

The background may be worked in Tent Stitch using one thread of Tapestry Wool, or Gobelin Filling (as shown) using four threads of Crewel Wool. For stitch details, see page 118.

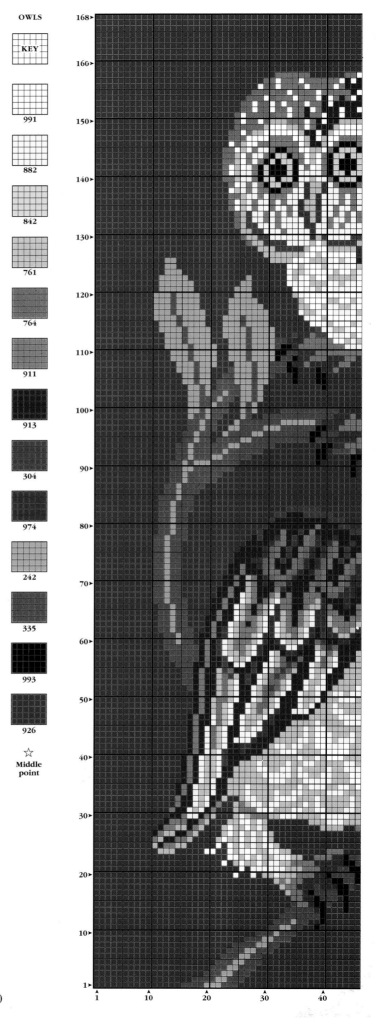

OWLS

KEY

991
882
842
761
764
911
913
304
974
242
335
993
926

☆
Middle point

RABBITS CUSHION

CANVAS: 12# to the inch (5# to the cm)

DESIGN AREA: 13 × 13 inches (33 × 33 cm)

STITCH: (Design) Tent, with 1 thread
(Background) Gobelin Filling or Tent

NEEDLE: Size 18

YARN: Appleton Tapestry Wool (Crewel or Tapestry for
background)

993 – 1 skein	762 – 2 skeins
972 – 1 skein	764 – 1 skein
913 – 1 skein	882 – 1 skein
984 – 2 skeins	241 – 4 skeins
989 – 1 skein	242 – 3 skeins
761 – 2 skeins	335 – 1 skein

Background: 926 – 3 hanks (Tapestry or Crewel)

These are quantities for the cushion cover shown.

The centre point shown on the chart is for working the
cushion.

Note that the greens are different from those in the rug:
353 on chart = 241, 355 = 242, 356 = 335.

The background may be worked in Tent Stitch using one
thread of Tapestry Wool, or Gobelin Filling (as shown)
using four threads of Crewel Wool. For stitch details, see
page 118. There is no border to the cushion, just the
background colour extended by two rows beyond the
design.

•

*The Rabbits, stitched on much coarser
canvas and with the design 'mirror-imaged' to form a charming rug.
The background has been altered to suit a child's room.*

93

RABBITS RUG

CANVAS: 6# to the inch (2½# to the cm)

DESIGN AREA: 28½ × 54 inches (72 × 137 cm)

STITCH: Cross, with 2 threads

NEEDLE: Size 16

YARN: Appleton Tapestry Wool

993 − 3 skeins
972 − 1 hank + 3 skeins
913 − 3 skeins
984 − 2 hanks
989 − 1 hank
761 − 4 hanks
762 − 3 hanks + 3 skeins
764 − 1 hank
882 − 3 skeins
353 − 7 hanks
355 − 4 hanks
356 − 1 hank
Background:
563 − 14 hanks
565 − 12 hanks

These are quantities for the rug shown.

The centre point shown on the chart is for the cushion. The centre of the rug is on the same line across, and on the far right-hand edge of the chart. The border shown on the chart is for the rug.

Note that the leaf greens and the background blues are different from those used in the cushion.

Mirror-imaging a design is easier for some people than for others. If you are keen to make the rug and find the problem too great, try taking a tracing of the first half when it has been worked and then retrace it in reverse on the other half of the canvas. It probably will not match stitch for stitch, but the fact that the outlines are correct will help with the colours.

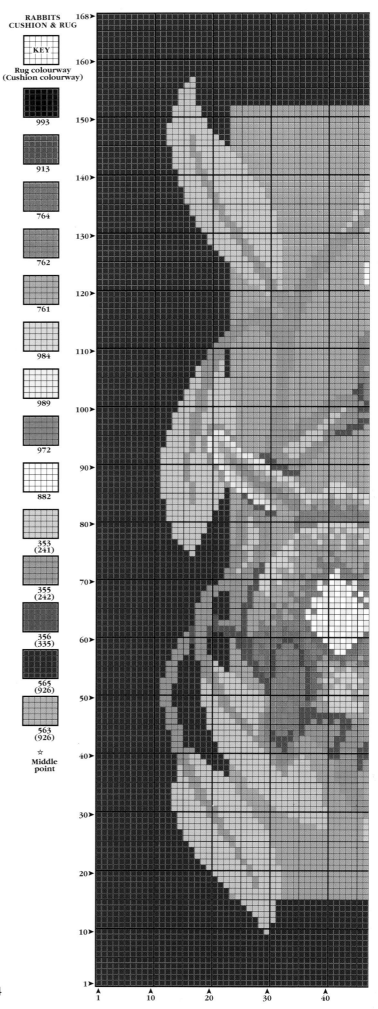

RABBITS
CUSHION & RUG

KEY

Rug colourway
(Cushion colourway)

993

913

764

762

761

984

989

972

882

353
(241)

355
(242)

356
(335)

565
(926)

563
(926)

☆
Middle
point

50   60   70   80   90   100   110   120   130   140   150   160   168

FROG & STORK

THIS IS ANOTHER of William De Morgan's amusing designs although, as with quite a lot of his work, there is just a hint of menace. I feel sure that there must be a proverb or a cautionary tale to go with it. The slight apprehension of the Frog and the deceptive sleepiness of the Stork seem to need an explanation – we want to know what has happened before and what is going to happen next. Perhaps there is a chance here for Granny to weave some magic for her grandchildren while she stitches.

The original tile was produced with many different backgrounds, but the bulrushes help to put it into a setting. Many of De Morgan's tiles were monochromatic and the colouring here, respectfully, is mine. The background gives a nice watery effect.

The stork actually looks like a cross between a Malibu stork and a heron; a real Malibu has an ugly red pouch under its beak and the heron, which does feed on frogs, has backswept head feathers. All in all it was better to stay as much as possible with the feel of the original as that was what De Morgan drew – anyway, I rather like the hairstyle!

I considered adding this to the Owls and Rabbits (page 88) to make a children's rug, but it was not similar enough in construction; it is upright, while the other two are rounder and might seem awkward with it.

The Frog is a strong enough character to make a cushion on his own. On 8#/inch (3#/cm) canvas he becomes 8½ inches (21.5 cm) tall. He is stitched in cross stitch using one strand of tapestry wool. Selina Winter felt that he looked a bit isolated, floating in air, so she stitched him sitting on a stone. He could be in the puddle shown on the chart, or even on a leaf; it's up to you.

This would be a good beginner's project for children. The coarse canvas means it can be completed quickly and the colours are complicated enough to be interesting yet simple enough not to be too daunting. The subject matter should make it fun.

•

The two cushions appropriately shown near water. The Frog on his own has been stitched on coarser canvas, thereby increasing his size. It looks as if this larger Frog is casting a protective eye on his younger brother, who seems slightly under threat from the Stork.

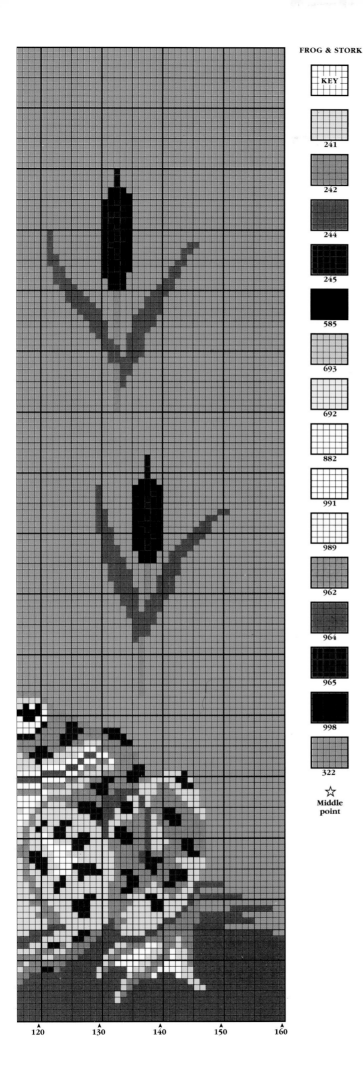

KEY

241

242

244

245

585

693

692

882

991

989

962

964

965

998

322

☆
Middle
point

FROG & STORK

FROG AND STORK CUSHION

CANVAS: 12# to the inch (5# to the cm)

DESIGN AREA: 14 × 14 inches (35.5 × 35.5 cm)

STITCH: Tent, with 1 thread

NEEDLE: Size 18

YARN: Appleton Tapestry Wool

241 − 1 skein		962 − 2 skeins	
242 − 1 skein		964 − 3 skeins	
244 − 1 skein		965 − 2 skeins	
245 − 1 skein		998 − 1 skein	
882 − 1 skein		991 − 1 skein	
585 − 1 skein		692 − 1 skein	
989 − 1 skein		693 − 1 skein	

Background: 322 − 2 hanks + 4 skeins

FROG CUSHION

CANVAS: 8# to the inch (3# to the cm)

DESIGN AREA: 8½ × 9 inches (21.5 × 23 cm)

STITCH: Cross, with 1 thread (see also page 114)

NEEDLE: Size 16

YARN: Appleton Tapestry Wool

241 − 2 skeins	882 − 1 skein
242 − 2 skeins	998 − 1 skein
244 − 1 skein	991 − 1 skein
245 − 1 skein	

Background (Appleton Crewel Wool):
568 − 3 hanks to make an area 13 inches (33 cm) square.

These are quantities for the two cushion covers shown.

The Frog on his own sits on a stone; mine is made up of one skein of Appleton Tapestry Wool 972 and three skeins of 974 but, you can use whatever colours and shape take your fancy. The background is worked with four threads of Appleton Crewel Wool as this gives better coverage over a plain area.

If you need to add to the design, or would just like to show more background, you will require more yarn − see page 113.

120　　130　　140　　150　　160

ANNIE JACK

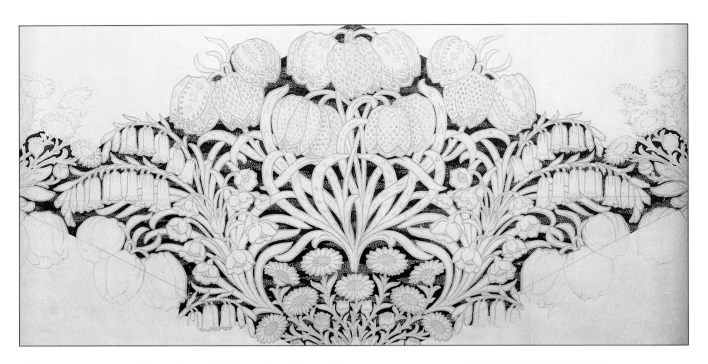

ANNIE JACK was the wife of William Morris's chief furniture designer and one of his main embroiderers. I have called these designs after her as it is believed that they were found in her house after her death; each is for a repeating fabric. I particularly wanted to see the many flowers in the large one in colour.

In 1990 I was fortunate enough to have an exhibition of my work in Japan as part of a large promotion of British design. It provided the perfect excuse for deciding on the threads and having the design stitched. The delicacy of Cross Stitch on linen seemed more suitable than canvaswork, although the restrictions imposed on the designer are the same for both.

The threads we used are Danish Flower Threads. I was not totally familiar with the colour range and unfortunately did not have enough time to try out variations before the exhibition. I would like to play with the yellows and greens in the large piece; you, with the design charted, are free to explore all the possibilities.

It would be interesting to use elements of this design separately – the daisies as a group or a stem of fritillaries. It was most enjoyable seeing it all come to life.

The two other antique drawings, which repeat a single flower, have a corner which had been painted. These two corners have been extracted from the overall design and stitched with Danish Flower Threads – the coral flower on linen and the yellow flower on dark-coloured Aida to imitate the painted background. Their simplicity is lovely and would work just as well on much coarser canvas.

ANNIE JACK

EVENWEAVE LINEN: 28# to the inch (11# to the cm)
OR AIDA: 14# to the inch (5½# to the cm)

STITCH: Cross, with 1 thread

NEEDLE: Size 22 or 24

YARN: Danish Flower Threads

LARGER PIECE (Linen):

DESIGN AREA: 14 × 24 inches (36 × 61 cm)

Fritillaries	Aconites	Bluebells	Daisy Petals	Leaves
3	6		0	
4	46		19	
11	203		101	
14	225		212	
29		21	238	
235		22	302	
		227		
		228		

•

The three designs found at the house of Annie Jack. She was the wife of Morris & Co's chief furniture designer, and also both designed and embroidered pieces for The Firm. These three are all repeating designs and would be suitable for printed fabrics.

The patches of colour from the two simpler designs have been reproduced as small cross-stitch pictures. The more complex design has been completely embroidered.

ANNIE JACK

KEY

| | 0 | 19 | 225 | 46 | 203 | 6 | 21 | 22 | 227 | 228 |

| 3 | 4 | 11 | 235 | 14 | 29 | 101 | 238 | 302 | 212 | ☆ Middle point |

104

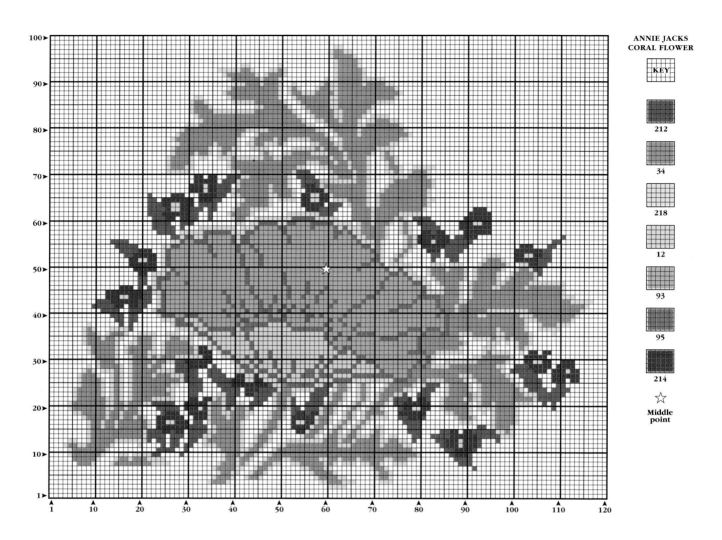

ANNIE JACKS
CORAL FLOWER

KEY

212

34

218

12

93

95

214

☆
Middle
point

SMALLER PIECES:

CORAL FLOWER (LINEN)

DESIGN AREA: 6½ × 7½ inches (16.5 × 19 cm)

YARN: Danish Flower Threads

12	212
34	214
93	218
95	

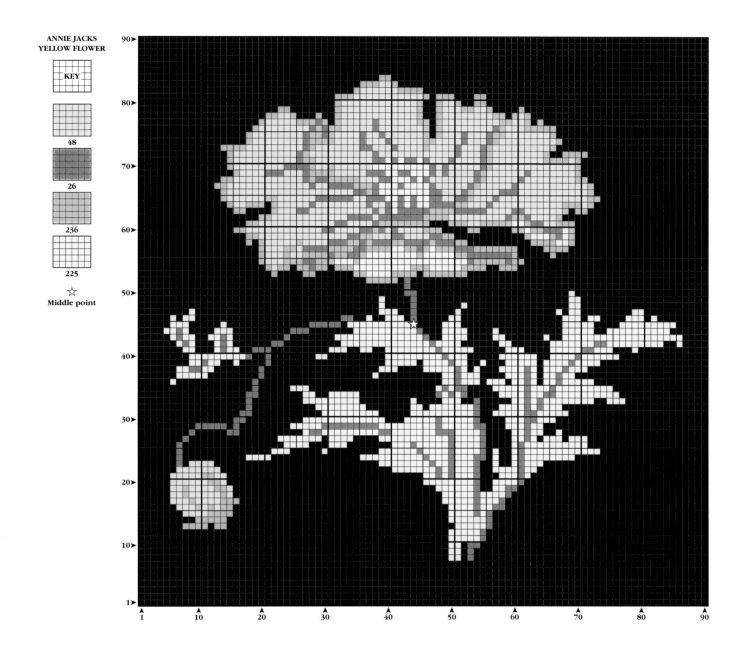

**ANNIE JACKS
YELLOW FLOWER**

KEY

48

26

236

225

☆
Middle point

YELLOW FLOWER (BLUE AIDA)

DESIGN AREA: 5½ × 6½ inches (14 × 16 cm)

YARN: Danish Flower Threads

26	225
48	236

Both designs are worked in Cross Stitch, either using one
thread over two intersections of the Linen or one thread
over one intersection of the Aida.

BIRD & LEAF

THIS PRETTY DESIGN, inspired by a silk and wool fabric created by C. F. A. Voysey in 1899, lends itself to more applications than most. Originally I had thought of it as a bolster cushion with just one more line of leaves. To do this you might omit the last blue bird on the right and replace it with the diving brown one on the far left and continue with that group.

The birds are rather varied in their sizes but are quite amusing and interchangeable. I have never seen the original Voysey version in colour and because his birds are very stylised, I have had to invent. House martins were chosen, with sand martins to give more variety to the colours. Each type flies in a group with an odd bird or two slightly out of formation and swooping to rejoin their friends. It was fascinating to play with the positioning of the birds and the arrangement of the colours.

All the design elements in Voysey's original are outlined, with an irregular striped background which gives the impression of waves of water or a hazy sky. I tried to retain this feel, but, as a background worked in Long Stitch has a tendency to obscure the edges of the design, I used the outlining to help the birds to stand out, working them in Tent Stitch with the darker of the background blues. Upon reflection, I think that the leaves could have benefitted from the same treatment.

The problem with the colour of the background was finding two blues which would give an illusion of sky or water; they needed to be close in shade but distinguishable from one another. The best solution was to use one solid colour for one stripe and to blend it with a lighter shade for the other.

Should you wish to make a bell pull, use the chart and replace the bottom leaf with the top one which gently twists into the centre leaf. The birds could be as they are in the right-hand fall of leaves, or they could be varied – with the chart you have complete freedom to experiment.

The design might also be used to make a very pretty curtain pelmet, either by using the leaves as they are (just the three central ones) and by adjusting the birds – or by twisting the design, again using one fall of leaves, this time horizontally, and adjusting the birds. You will need to count carefully to make sure that the birds you have chosen will fit or perhaps overlap the leaves. They will of course need to be flying horizontally!

•

Stylised birds are a recurring theme in Voysey's work; mine are more realistic and colourful. They look as if they are flying to freedom.

BIRD & LEAF CUSHION

CANVAS: 14# to the inch (5½# to the cm)

DESIGN AREA: 13 × 13 inches (33 × 33 cm)

STITCH: Tent, with 3 threads (see also page 114)

NEEDLE: Size 20

YARN: Appleton Crewel Wool

873	– 2 skeins	852	– 1 skein
874	– 2 skeins	929	– 2 skeins
352	– 5 skeins	926	– 2 skeins
401	– 5 skeins	993	– 1 skein
293	– 2 skeins	882	– 1 skein
294	– 2 skeins	588	– 1 skein
762	– 2 skeins	986	– 1 skein
991b	– 1 skein	185	– 2 skeins
974	– 1 skein	187	– 1 skein

Background:
876 – 4 skeins   561 – 1 hank + 4 skeins

These are quantities for the cushion cover shown.

One row of Tent Stitch in 561 is worked around the birds to give them a clearly defined outline.

Stitch the whites of the eyes last, using white sewing cotton on top of the black stitches.

The background is worked in alternate rows, blending 1 thread of 561 and 2 of 876 in the needle for one row and 3 threads of 561 on its own for the next (see page 120).

Three rows of Tent Stitch in 561 are worked around the whole design.

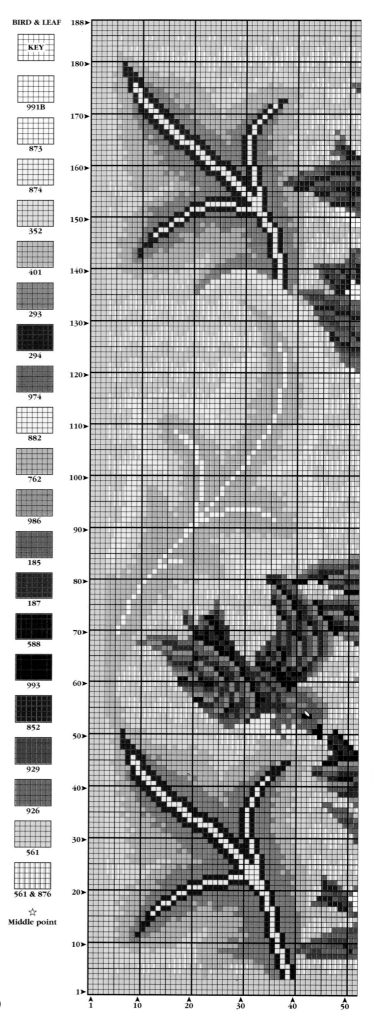

BASIC
TECHNIQUES

HOPEFULLY YOU NOW feel enthusiastic about starting a new project. My aim is that, even if you decide to start on the simplest piece and not alter anything from my original, you will soon be confident enough to adapt and change as much as I know I would.

Choose carefully – preferably something you need, something that will enhance your decor – or maybe decide on a gift (but only for someone who will appreciate it). It has to be something that you will really want to complete.

This decision will need to be followed by others: the size and then the colours. With this fairly broad picture, you move on to the fun of buying the materials. At this stage you might prefer to buy small quantities and try them out. If you are intending to change anything drastically, especially the colours, I would strongly recommend some experimentation.

The basic steps, after you have decided on your design and its purpose, are as follows:

(a) assessing the correct gauge and size of canvas or other fabric (see page 116 for calculating sizes from charts)
(b) choosing the most suitable threads, both type and colour
(c) finding the correct needle
(d) understanding charts
(e) marking the background
(f) deciding whether you wish to use a frame and which kind
(g) stitching and how to start and finish
(h) finishing your stitched work
(i) the moment of truth – its final display.

All of these points are discussed in the pages that follow. I hope that they do not sound too much like a teaching manual, but it is important to be disciplined in your choices at the outset – for instance, nothing is more demoralising than putting in several hours of stitching only to discover that the piece of canvas you have been using is too small. That happened to me – but only once.

Remember that your project is unique; only you have stitched it. A small deviation from the way that I have done things is not necessarily a mistake; instead it is your own personal contribution to the finished piece. There is no 'totally wrong' nor 'totally right' way in these matters, only enjoyment. If you are not enjoying what you are doing, you need to rethink it. Perhaps you can find a simpler way to complete the piece, or choose more inspiring colours.

MATERIALS

CANVAS AND FABRIC

CANVAS Most of the pieces in this book have been stitched on canvas, either single or rug interlock. For my kits, I prefer to use high-quality polished deluxe single canvas, both because its smoothness does not roughen the threads and because of its strength. If a canvas is badly out of shape after stitching, as sometimes happens, the stretching of the dampened finished canvas will need to be quite drastic; weak canvas can tear. Rug canvas is inherently quite heavy and strong; the stretching here should be minimal as I advocate Cross Stitch for all my rugs to limit distortion.

Canvas comes in different widths and thread counts (#). The more threads there are to the inch (cm), the more stitches to the inch (cm). Thus, a finer canvas will take longer to stitch, but will enable you to show more detail. The finer the canvas, of course, the finer the thread needed to stitch it.

Always buy the best quality canvas that you can afford – your time is the most valuable part of any work – and make sure that it is large enough to accommodate your design.

SIZE Decide at the outset what size you want your finished piece to be. Whether this is the same as the samples that I have shown, or whether you want to extend the background (see Wools below) to make a larger cushion or a special shape such as a chair seat, you will need at least 2 inches (5cm) all round your chosen stitched area to allow for 'stretching' or 'blocking' when you have finished.

Remember, if you choose a gauge of canvas that is coarser than that used for the samples, the design will finish up larger and you will need an appropriate piece of canvas to accommodate it. See below for how to calculate.

LINEN Linen has been used with several of the designs to show how different a design can look on another medium.

The type of linen produced for counted embroidery is called 'evenweave'. It has the same number of warp and weft threads to the inch (or cm). The weave is like single canvas, though the threads are never absolutely smooth and usually have a natural slub. It is available in different gauges, all rather fine, of which 28# to the inch (11# to the cm) is probably the most commonly used.

As the background is rarely stitched and as linen is slightly transparent, threads at the back can be seen from the front of the work. It is therefore important that the thread is finished off after each block of stitching. The fabric is much softer than canvas, so it is easier to work on a frame.

AIDA This is a cotton fabric, the threads of which are woven very evenly; this makes it ideally suited for counted work. Cross Stitch is made over one intersection. It is not as see-through as linen or canvas, as the fabric is somewhat denser.

It is still not advisable, especially with lighter coloured Aida, to run threads across the back between the stitching. Again, a frame is a good idea to keep the fabric taut.

WASTE CANVAS This is a loose evenweave fabric with fine threads. Its purpose is to enable you to transfer a counted design onto an otherwise unsuitable fabric. A piece of the canvas is tacked lightly onto the main fabric where the design is to be placed. The stitches are counted from a chart in the normal way, but the needle must pass through the canvas hole (not snagging the canvas) and through the fabric underneath. Pull the thread slightly tighter than usual. When complete, the canvas threads and tacking are gently withdrawn, leaving the design miraculously on your suede collar or silk shirt.

WOOLS AND COTTONS

All my thinking is done in Appleton colours. Years of familiarity have made it easy to identify which Appleton number will most closely resemble the shade I am looking for. Therefore, all the wools in these designs are the same make – if you prefer to use, or can more easily find another brand of wool, there are conversion charts available from the manufacturers, and embroidery shops usually have shade cards showing samples.

Both Appleton Crewel and Tapestry Wools come in the same range of numbered colours.

CREWEL WOOL is 2-ply fine wool suitable for any gauge of canvas and necessary for finer canvas such as 18# or 14# and for blending colours. Many believe, too, that because several threads need to be used at the same time in the needle, this wool lies flatter than Tapestry Wool.

TAPESTRY WOOL is a thicker 4-ply, usually used as a single thread (unless you are working on a very coarse canvas). The thickness is equivalent to 3 threads of Crewel; its advantage is that you only need to thread one through the needle. The disadvantage is that the subtle blending of shades is not possible and if a different stitch is being used for the background it might not cover the canvas.

Appleton wools are sold in hanks (about 1 ounce/25 grams) or smaller skeins. As a general guide, one hank will cover 36 square inches (232 square cms) or 6 × 6 inches (15 × 15 cm) working in tent stitch on 18#, 14# or 12# to the inch canvas (7#, 5½# or 5# to the cm). I prefer to work using hanks, as they are easily cut to the ideal length – about 30 inches (76 cm) for stitching.

If you wish to increase the size of your project by working on a larger gauge of canvas, increasing the background area or adding a border, you will need more wool than specified. Ideally it is best to learn your own needs by noting how much you cover with a particular stitch on your chosen canvas with a measured length of wool. (If you have not done any stitching before, use the method above and try to note if the specified amount is correct for you.)

To allow for any dye changes, it is advisable to get all your background wool at the same time. If you cannot do this, make sure that you do not run out completely. Then some of the original purchase can be blended with the new in the needle for a few rows, making the change so gradual as to be unnoticeable. This is, of course, not possible if you are using only one thread of Tapestry Wool in your needle.

As you can see, it is a matter of trying for yourself. The instructions for each design state what was actually used, but it may not suit you.

It is always best, after you have bought your canvas and before deciding on the threads, to try a few stitches to see how your tension covers the canvas. This will help you decide if you want Crewel or Tapestry Wool and if you are working out your own colour scheme, you will certainly need to stitch the shades together to see if they work as you expected. Stitched threads have a quite different effect on each other from ones that you just hold in the hand. The Owls and Rabbits with their two shades of background prove that!

COTTONS Out of the very many different sorts and makes available, I have contented myself with just two – both sold in skeins. Stranded Cotton (called Floss in America) comes in a large range of colours from several manufacturers. They are all six-stranded threads and have a sheen rather like silk. Danish Flower Threads have a limited, but surprisingly versatile range of soft colours reminiscent of the vegetable dyes once used to make them. They are single-stranded and soft-textured with no sheen.

NEEDLES

Blunt-ended tapestry needles with long, easily threaded eyes are best. Size 16 is suitable for rug canvas and will take two threads of Tapestry Wool if needed. Size 18 is best for 12#/inch (5#/cm) canvas; size 20 for 14#/inch (5½#/cm) and size 22 for 18#/inch (7#/cm). The rule of thumb is that the needle should be easy to thread with the appropriate amount of yarn and easy to pull through the canvas.

To thread a needle, fold the threads around the needle and pinch tight; slide them off the needle while still pinching them and push the fold of threads through the eye.

NUMBER OF THREADS

Again, with each set of instructions, I have specified the number of threads that I used in the needle to cover the canvas or to achieve the blending that was required. However, different stitchers work with different tensions; some pull more tightly than others and this can affect the thickness

of the thread needed. There are a few golden rules that might help.

The thread(s) should pull easily through the canvas with no tugging needed and, when a block of stitches has been completed, no canvas should be 'grinning' through. If you can achieve this and a nice even tension, you are on your way to excellence. The tension is the key to all this. A tight tension will, of course, pull the wool and cause it to be thinner; a too-tight tension might distort the canvas unless it is well framed. Professionals who work very fast on very taut frames tend to have a tight tension – they will always need the maximum thickness of thread to cover the canvas. A newcomer working in the hand needs to avoid pulling too tightly, so many find a thinner thread adequate to cover their canvas. It is up to each stitcher to decide as an individual.

The gauge of canvas used for my designs that is most open to discussion is 14#/inch (5½#/cm). Many people use three threads of Crewel Wool (or one of Tapestry); others find this too tight and are happier with two threads of Crewel. Working in Cross Stitch on 8#/inch (3# cm), some are happier with one thread of Tapestry Wool, others with four threads of Crewel.

The thickness of the thread is also affected by the type of stitch. A straight stitch over, say, four intersections of canvas will need a thicker thread to cover it than Tent Stitch on the same canvas. You may therefore, if you have chosen Tapestry Wool for the design, need to use Crewel for the background, where an extra thread can easily be added for the long stitch. Do not worry about using some Tapestry Wool and some Crewel on the same piece – you will not notice the difference.

Here is a table of canvas gauges, wools and stitches used in this book.

NUMBER OF THREADS IN THE NEEDLE

CANVAS	TENT STITCH	CROSS STITCH	STRAIGHT STITCH
18#/inch 7#/cm	2 crewel		3 crewel or 1 tapestry
14#/inch 5½#/cm	2 crewel or 3 crewel or 1 tapestry		4 crewel
12#/inch 5#/cm	3 crewel or 1 tapestry		5 crewel or 6 crewel
8#/inch★ 3#/cm	6 crewel or 2 tapestry	4 crewel or 1 tapestry	8 crewel or 3 tapestry
6#/inch★ 2½#/cm		8 crewel or 2 tapestry	

★ Tent Stitch and Straight Stitch, although possible on these coarser canvases, both require a lot of threads in the needle.

STITCHING

This can be done by using either one or both hands. If a frame is used, the needle can be passed through the canvas from one hand to the other, forming a stitch each time it travels up and down. This can be done incredibly quickly by experienced stitchers and people used to this technique are generally reluctant to change. Sometimes one hand is used to insert the needle and the same hand used to pull it out under the work and replace it. As the hand has to move from over to under the canvas continuously, it is a slow method. A faster way to stitch with one hand is better done without a frame, as the canvas needs to be pliable. Each placing of the needle inserts it into one hole and, in the same movement, out of the next. The hand needs only to move to the pointed end of the needle to extract it, then repeat the movement. This is very useful for the middle of large pieces where getting both hands and arms around yards of canvas can be exhausting. A word of warning about this last method: try not to pull too tightly. The canvas is already slightly bent by the action of the needle entering and leaving at the same time – if you pull, you will distort the canvas. Just keep the action gentle and the tension even. After a while, you will slip into a rhythm which will make it much easier.

The order of stitching is important. It is advisable not to work the background until you are sure that the foreground details are correct. On printed canvases, it is crucial. The overlying parts of the design must be stitched first to give them clear outlines. I like to be able to work colours as I get to them and find it quicker and much less distracting if I have several needles threaded with different colours ready at the same time.

STARTING AND FINISHING

It is neater (and you'll find it easier) if the threads are finished off at the back by being held down by other stitches. An easy way to achieve this is to knot the thread and take it down from the right side of the canvas an inch or so away from

The front of this canvas looks impeccable!

where you will start. Position the knot so that you will be working towards it with the same or similar coloured yarn. You will find that, when you reach the knot, the thread will be woven in behind and the knot can safely be cut off. You can finish off similarly by bringing the end of the thread up a little distance from your work and, when you have stitched up to it, it too will be tightly woven in. To thread through the stitches at the back has the same effect, but it means turning the canvas over – not always easy on a frame.

Knots on the wrong side of your work have two disadvantages. One is that they sometimes get entangled with your stitching, which is a nuisance; also they might cause bumps on the right side when your work is finished and stretched.

CHARTS

For those who already favour following charts (rather than stitching onto a painted or printed canvas), I have nothing to say. To the uninitiated, I must warn you that stitching from charts can become an addiction!

All the charts in this book have been produced by Ethan Danielson, whose wizardry with the computer has given us both the beauty of art and the precision of science. Each colour on the chart represents one colour of wool and each square represents one stitch.

It is always best to start working in good daylight. Sort the wools and identify which square in the index they represent. If the colours are very close – they inevitably are in Fox, for instance – note in the good daylight where they are positioned.

Find the centre mark on the chart (normally this will correspond with the centre of the canvas, but see the paragraph below). Find the canvas centre by folding it in half each way – the intersection is the centre. I prefer to mark these intersecting lines by tacking along them with bright sewing cotton as it helps to dissect the chart and give more points of reference from which to count.

Not everyone likes to start from the centre. If you do not, it is essential to make sure that the design is going to fit within your chosen canvas area. It is possible that the centre of the canvas is not where you will want to place the centre of the design – in the case of a chair seat with a larger drop at the front than the back, for instance, you will want the design to appear in the centre of the seat – or, possibly, a repeat of the design will be called for on a long stool – or, with Woodpecker, if you only want to use part of the design to fit a squarer shape. Whatever your chosen design, careful planning pays enormous dividends.

The boon of charts is their versatility. You can, of course, follow the exact formula given in the book and you will know how your finished work should look. But, more importantly with a chart, you can adapt the design to your precise needs. In this book I hope that I have given you a small taste of what can be achieved.

The design size may be reduced or increased by changing the gauge of the canvas, by increasing or eliminating the background, by adding borders or by extending the design itself (as with the Fox and Hare chair seats). The colouring can be changed, as can the actual materials used – and, naturally, you need only stitch the part you like best.

To calculate how a design will alter its size on a different canvas, take the number of stitches on the chart and divide that number by the gauge of the canvas; this will give you the eventual size. For example, 140 stitches will measure 14 inches on a 10#/inch canvas (35 cm on 4#/cm). On an 18#inch canvas it will measure just under 8 inches (20 cm on 7#/cm).

$$\frac{\text{Number of Stitches}}{\text{Gauge of Canvas}} = \text{Size of Design} \quad \frac{140}{10} = 14$$

Do not forget the extra plain canvas you will need around the design.

On linen the same principle applies, but if you use Cross Stitch over two intersections it effectively halves the gauge – a 28#/inch (11#/cm) linen counts as 14# (5½#). Therefore, the same design with 140 stitches will measure 10 inches (25 cm) if worked in Cross Stitch over two intersections of 28#/inch (11#/cm) linen and 5 inches (12.5 cm) if Tent Stitch is used over one intersection.

SPECIAL SHAPES

After choosing the canvas, check carefully that you have enough threads in both directions to accommodate the number of stitches in your design (plus the 2 inches (5 cm) all round for stretching). If you are making an unusually shaped piece you will also need to mark out the background area before you start. It is not necessary if you have just decided to work a few rows around the design in straight lines, but if the area is curved or if you need to leave some parts unstitched so that it will sit well around the leg of a stool, it is almost impossible to do this accurately at a later stage – either because the canvas is on a frame or because it has already gone a little out of shape.

TEMPLATES

A good upholsterer can make a template for you; this is simply a piece of paper or cloth (muslin or calico are perfect) cut to the exact shape you need to cover with your stitching, so it is not too difficult to do yourself. The outline should be drawn onto the canvas before you do anything else. If a piece of furniture is being re-covered, it is possible to use the old cover as a template. Any re-upholstering or re-stuffing should be done before you establish the final shape so, if you use the old fabric, check that it is still the right size. Lay the fabric over the area to be covered, smooth the cloth flat,

The Hare chair seat (see pages 26/27), showing the extra stitching and shape required

hold in place with pins and mark with a pencil where your stitching will need to end. Mark around legs which protrude into the design area. Mark where you want the centre of your design to fall.

Remove the template, check the lines are symmetrical (often simply by folding it in half) and, if not, check the upholstery again before cutting along the line you have drawn. Lay the template on the canvas and make sure the canvas threads follow the vertical and horizontal lines of the template. This ensures that the design will not be lop-sided. Make sure, too, that the centre mark of the template is also marked onto the canvas as this is where you will want the centre of the design to lie. If you are going to stitch two designs on a long stool, for instance, you might want to count the threads before deciding exactly where the centres of the designs should be.

Mark the canvas around the edges of the template – either with a running stitch in coloured sewing thread or with an indelible pen. Your background needs to be stitched to this line. However, the canvas should be, even at the closest points, 2 inches (5 cm) or more all round. The canvas must not be cut until the stitching and stretching are done and then, ideally, by your upholsterer.

FRAMES

Some of the advantages of working on a frame will have become apparent from the stitching section above. Frames hold the work flat and under tension so that both hands can be used to stitch. They also help the work to retain a better shape, making the stretching procedure, when the work is finished, easier.

There are many ways of framing, from the traditional

116

Slate Frame which allows the canvas to be held very tightly, to attaching the canvas to an old picture frame with drawing pins. In theory the width of the frame should be wider than the total width of the unworked canvas. In a Slate Frame, where the canvas is sewn to tapes attached to the top and bottom bars, the canvas should not be wider than the length of the tape. If the width is correct (the canvas can be narrower) the length does not matter as it can be rolled around one of the bars at the top or bottom.

For very large pieces such as a rug, where you might find a full-sized frame impractical, the canvas can be pinned to a smaller frame so that the part to be worked is within the frame area; when a section is completed, the canvas can be moved and re-pinned. This can be done with a Slate Frame, an old picture frame or a Stretcher Frame. You will not get the canvas very tight but it means you will be able to use both hands; loose canvas should be rolled to enable you to reach under the frame.

A Round Frame can be used for smaller or larger projects. Again, the frame is moved from one part of the canvas or fabric to another. It can be difficult to fit partially worked canvas pieces onto a Round Frame as they can be stiff. However, with a little perseverance, it can be done, though it should be removed when you have finished stitching for the day. The larger the ring, the easier it is to accommodate coarser gauges of canvas.

Round Frames, also called Hoops, consist of two rings, one of them expandable by means of a screw or spring. The fabric is laid across the smaller ring and, with the screw loosened sufficiently, the larger one is pressed over the fabric and around the under ring; the screw is then tightened. The fabric may need to be pulled gently from the edges to ensure

it is taut, before the screw is made very tight. You can obtain Round Frames just as rings or with a mechanism to attach them to a table or floorstand.

Square frames can be found in varying weights from the strong Slate Frame to much lighter Travelling Frames – they work on the same principle, but you will not be able to achieve the same degree of tightness on a Travelling Frame.

There are now many forms of stands for both Square and Round frames. Some are very elegant pieces of furniture; others resemble something invented by Heath Robinson or Emmett, with joints and bolts everywhere to make the stand more adjustable to each person's needs.

Before you choose, it is obviously ideal if you can try one, or at least sit with it so that you can feel the weight; imagine where you will keep it at home. Many good embroidery shops will have one or two set up.

FIXING YOUR CANVAS TO A FRAME

How a Round Frame works is described above. Round Frames are ideal for linen or Aida – extremely easy to use and light in weight.

A Travel or lightweight Square Frame needs to have the canvas attached to the webbing at top and bottom; the webbing must be wider than the canvas. Find the centre of the webbing – match it with the centre of the canvas and hem stitch in place. The side bars are never very long and you will almost always have to roll the canvas around the bars at top or bottom, depending on which part of the canvas you are working on. The rollers are held to the bars by wing nuts; these tend to slip so it is not possible to hold the canvas very tight.

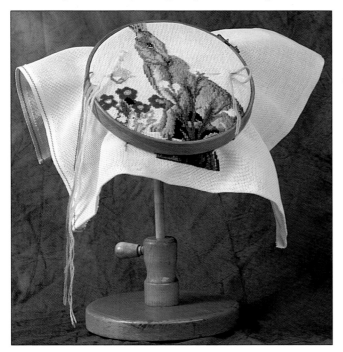

Table-standing round frame

Square slate frame

With a Slate Frame you can stretch the canvas very tightly as it can be pulled in both directions. Sew a strip of webbing along the two sides of canvas – do not hem the canvas as this will cause a thickness along the edge which will prevent the canvas from pulling tight when it is rolled. The webbing can be machine stitched if you wish. Match the centre of the top and bottom of the canvas to the centres of the webbing attached to the frame rollers. Fold the canvas back and stitch from the centre to the sides very firmly with button thread. It is important that the frame holds the canvas absolutely square, or it will simply cause you to stitch it out of shape.

When you have inserted the side slats into the rollers, see that the pegs are in the same position on each side – the holes are evenly spaced. You may need to roll the canvas around either the top or bottom roller bar (Woodpecker, for instance, would certainly need to be rolled). Similarly, see that the pegs are in the same holes on each side. Attach string very securely by tying to the top of the side slat and roller and, using a large-eyed needle, loop the string at regular intervals around the side slat and through the webbing. Pull very tightly and attach securely. This stringing may have to be removed and replaced as you reposition the canvas to complete the stitching. It can be drum-tight and, once you have stitched well-framed canvas using both hands, you will understand why many people are prepared to go to all this trouble.

TYPES OF STITCHES

For each of the main worked samples throughout this book, I have specified which type of stitch was used. The most common of these are Tent Stitch for those worked on finer canvas such as the cushions and chair seats, and Cross Stitch where coarser canvas is used for such items as rugs. Cross Stitch is also used for the alternative examples worked on linen – see below.

Interesting effects can often be achieved by using more decorative 'long' stitches for the background areas; Gobelin Filling is one that I have used, but there are several books devoted entirely to the many types of canvas work stitches.

TENT STITCH

This is a diagonal stitch, which forms a long stitch on the back of the canvas. It has the advantage of being a small stitch; as it goes over only one thread of the canvas, design details can be depicted easily and it will wear well. It has the disadvantage, since it pulls only in one direction, of distorting the shape of the canvas. This means that you will need to stretch your work before making it up into a finished piece.

It may be stitched horizontally across the canvas back-

wards and forwards or down and up if you wish. If you are not using a frame, you can turn the canvas at the end of a row so that you always work from right to left or top to bottom (reverse if you are left-handed). If you are using a frame and both hands, there is no need to turn the canvas; just return along the next row, still putting the needle up through the stitch hole above and putting it down through the hole below and diagonally to the left. Continue along the row from left to right.

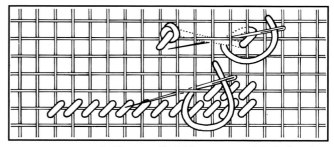

TENT STITCH worked horizontally (with canvas turned for 2nd row)

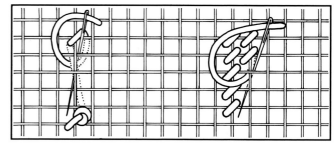

TENT STITCH worked vertically (with canvas turned for 2nd row)

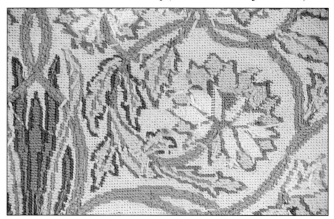

The back of diagonal tent stitch

Tent Stitch may also be worked in diagonal lines; this method is also called 'basketweave'. This distorts the canvas much less and gives a very firm back to your work and I would recommend it for backgrounds as it also gives a smooth finish. It is essential that you work alternately from top to bottom and then the reverse. Two rows in the same direction cause a break in the weave at the back which will show on the front. To help you remember in which direction the last row was worked, always leave a thread hanging from your last stitch.

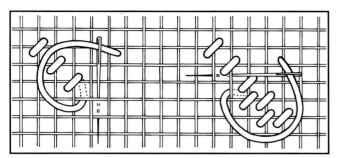

BASKETWEAVE

The back of basketweave

Half-Cross Stitch gives the same appearance on the front, but has a short stitch on the back. It is really suitable only for interlock canvas which will not allow the stitches to slip between the weave, which can happen with normal single canvas.

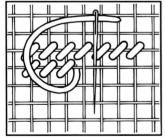

HALF CROSS STITCH   *CROSS STITCH*

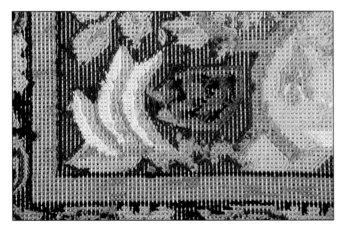

The back of a cross-stitch rug showing the short stitch on the back

CROSS STITCH

This has been used for all the rugs in the book. It has the advantages of being hard wearing as well as helping the canvas hold its shape since there are pulls in opposite directions with each stitch.

There are many ways of executing the stitch. All are correct, but you must find the one that suits you best. The most usual way is to work the required number of stitches in Half-Cross, then return along them completing the crosses. Most people also use Half-Cross Stitch for the second part of the cross, so that only a short stitch can be seen at the back of the work. However, others are happier with Tent Stitch as the second row. This gives both a long stitch and a good padding on the back, but may pull the canvas unevenly, causing it to need stretching. Other people prefer to complete each individual cross before starting the next, either using the methods described above, or by placing the needle both in and out of the canvas in one horizontal movement.

No matter which method you use, it is imperative that all the top stitches lie in the same direction to give a smooth and professional look.

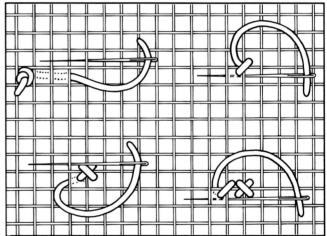

CROSS STITCH worked in one movement

The back of a cross-stitch rug showing the long stitch on the back

CROSS STITCH ON LINEN

As linen is not an interlocked fabric, it is important that the stitches do not slide between the threads. To avoid this, Cross Stitch is normally worked over two intersections.

Remember too, when calculating the eventual size of your work, that stitching across two intersections of 28# count linen will give the same finished design size as stitching across one intersection of 14# canvas.

GOBELIN FILLING/BRICK STITCH

This gives a pleasant padded look to a background. It was used in the OWLS and RABBITS cushions. As the background meets the main design, the stitches need to be shortened accordingly – also, of course, at the top and bottom the 'fill-in' stitches will be over two threads of the canvas, not four. It is extremely simple and quick; however, you will need more threads to cover the canvas than you use for Tent Stitch. Try one extra thread of crewel wool – if it does not cover, add another – until you are satisfied the canvas will not show through.

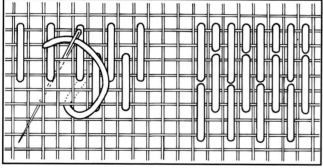

GOBELIN FILLING/BRICK STITCH

BACKGROUND FOR BIRD & LEAF (page 108) This is exactly like Brick Stitch, although I decided to go over three threads: make two stitches next to each other, then step down for one stitch, step down again for the next two, then up for the next and up for the next, giving a wavy effect. One row was stitched using one colour and the next a mixture of two.

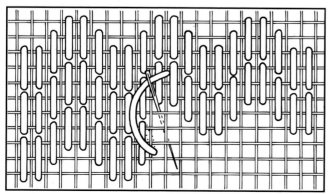

BRICK STITCH worked over 3 threads

STRETCHING

When the happy day arrives . . . the last stitch placed . . . the thread made secure . . . you view your finished work . . . you are only part-way to the full satisfaction that you are going to achieve. Whether or not your work of art is out of shape (and very few are not), it will genuinely benefit from 'stretching' or 'blocking'.

My firm belief is that this is a much more difficult thing to do than many people think. A professionally stretched cushion cover will have absolutely straight sides and perfectly right-angled corners. However, here are the principles; with quite a bit of practice you may reach a high standard. Incidentally, linen is normally stitched on a frame; gentle ironing on the wrong side with the linen resting on a padded board is all that should be necessary.

Canvas is a pliable medium; the act of stitching can, and usually does, pull it out of shape. Diagonal stitches are most likely to do this. Stretching serves two purposes: the first is to return the canvas to its original shape, the second is that it gives the worked piece a crisp, nicely 'finished' look – much as ironing will improve the look of a tablecloth, even if it is only slightly creased. Just ironing your canvas work will not give the same effect, however.

There is now special equipment available for stretching. There are stretcher boards, used a great deal in the USA, which consist of a square of hardboard marked with lines and drilled with holes at regular intervals and supplied with stainless nails. There are also racking machines which have pins that grip the edges of the canvas and will pull it out until straight, and I am sure there are others that I have not heard of. If you do not have any of these, you need a clean board into which you can hammer nails (and remove them fairly easily). It has to be larger than the piece you are stretching. You also need carpet tacks or stainless steel nails, pliers, a hammer, a set-square . . . and a great deal of determination!

All pieces are stretched square or rectangular – not cut into any special shape. A template, if you have one, can be used to check the shape as you stretch.

Cut the selvedge off your worked piece and machine a narrow hem all round. It must be strong as it is where you will put the nails or tacks.

If the piece is not very much out of shape, it can be easier to handle dry. If it needs dampening, I find that it is easier to wrap it in a wet tea towel for a few minutes; do not soak. In case the board contains anything that might run onto the damp canvas, it should be covered securely with blotting paper or a clean cloth.

The aim is to tack the worked piece, right side down, onto the board so that all the canvas threads are running straight and at right angles to each other. It is called 'stretching' simply because you will not achieve this unless you do stretch the canvas (and stretch it quite hard). People have different pet ways of placing the tacks – they need to be about ½ inch (1.25 cm) apart, or closer. If you have marked the centres of each side of the canvas and have a way of lining them up on the board (by measuring or pre-marking), you can nail the four centres or the corners. Or you can start with one side and its adjacent side and continue around. You will almost certainly need to remove the tacks continually and replace them until you are happy that the piece is absolutely square and very taut. If you have not pulled it enough, it will just bubble out of shape again as it dries. If you did not dampen beforehand, or even if you did, you can lay a damp cloth on top of the piece and very lightly iron over it (do not press). This steams the work and, if it is dry, helps it move into the new shape. The drying is what sets it. It is absolutely essential that it is left until it is totally dry, which will be at least 24 hours (48 is safer).

There are varying viewpoints on the use of coatings to make the work hold its shape after being made up. If your stitching is likely to be subjected to any damp surroundings, it will start to return to the original stitched shape it had before being stretched; this would be a strong reason to use a weak solution of anti-fungicidal wallpaper paste on the back to help hold it. Other solutions are sold for this purpose; check with your needlework supplier or a local picture framer who knows about finishing needlework. Many embroidery shops can arrange stretching and making up, so it is always worth asking. They can probably show you samples of what they have done and discuss your particular project with you.

You should now understand why you needed the extra unworked canvas all round your stitching. If you do not, for some reason, have enough, then strong cloth tape can be machine stitched around the edges (preferably before work-ing) to take the place of the canvas.

MAKING UP

As with 'Finishing Off' I often feel that, after all the efforts of stitching, a special finish done by a professional seems a small investment. However, to do it yourself . . .

CUSHIONS

Cushions come in an almost endless range of shapes and sizes. Those in this book are either piped, corded or have an inset. Jasmine (page 61) is an example of what I call an inset, but it's a cheat! The stitched model was stretched, trimmed and slip-stitched onto the centre of one side of a ready-made cushion before the filling was added.

For the corded cushions you will need a filling 10 per cent larger than the stitched area of canvas and a backing material 2 inches (5 cm) larger – I like velvet or heavy silk; a cord to fit all the way around the cushion plus ½ yard/metre extra for knots or twists if you want them. Trim the stretched canvas to about 1 inch (2.5 cm) all round. Place

this and the backing material right sides together and tack carefully on three sides and along part of the fourth side, taking in each corner. With the stitching facing you, machine stitch following your tacking, keeping as close to your stitching line as possible. If you lightly hand stitch the canvas edges back and mitre the corners it will give your cushion a better shape. Turn inside out. Hand stitch the cord in place – knotting the corners as you go and ensuring that the cushion corners are pulled right out. Insert the padding. Slip stitch the gap left at the bottom.

For cushions piped with the backing fabric, you will need plain piping cord long enough to go around the cushion plus 1 inch (2.5 cm) for joining and enough extra backing fabric to enable you to cut strips on the bias (diagonally across the fabric) 2 inches (5 cm) wide and long enough to cover all the cord. The strips have to be cut on the cross as the fabric will stretch in that direction and allow you to form the corners of the cushion without bunching. Trim the worked canvas 1 inch (2.5 cm) outside your stitching all around; cut the backing fabric to the same size. Cut the strips of fabric for piping. Join them, also on the diagonal, by machine stitching them. Tack the piping fabric neatly around to cover the cord; place the covered cord between the embroidery and the backing fabric as they lie right sides together. The piping must be on the 'inside', out of sight. Tack very carefully so that the piping will lie tight up against your embroidery. Tack around the top, both sides and along the bottom a little way after turning the corners – leave a space in the middle of the bottom to insert the pad. If you have a piping foot, you can machine stitch following your tacking; otherwise a careful backstitch by hand will ensure a good finish. Turn the cover right side out and make sure the corners are square. Insert the pad and slip stitch the opening on the bottom edge to finish it.

RUGS

As already stated, all canvas work benefits from stretching even if it is not really out of shape. If you are not going to have this done professionally, you will need a large board or old table or wooden floor that you do not mind making holes in. Failing all, you can press it lightly with a steam iron on the reverse side. I must be honest and confess that not all my rugs have been stretched, but they are straight and soft and comfortable.

Many rug makers like to give their rugs a good finish by turning under the unworked canvas and making the last row of stitches around the outside of the rug through the two layers. This does give a very neat edge but makes stretching impossible – so stretch yours before this stage.

LINING Rugs that are intended as wall-hangings or throws for sofas need a much lighter lining than those which will be walked on. For a light lining you need a strong thread, a long strong sharp needle and a suitable lining fabric, perhaps something you might use for heavy curtains. For a heavy lining you will need a thin but firm, good quality felt for interlining and a stronger outer lining such as hessian, Union cloth or Holland. The felt should be exactly the same size as the worked area of the rug. The other linings need an extra 4–6 inches (10–15 cm) so that 2–3 inches (5–7 cm) may be turned under all round.

First trim the excess canvas all round the rug to within 2–3 inches (5–7.5 cm) of the worked area. Pinch it firmly back so that no raw canvas shows on the right side of the rug – pin and secure it with herringbone stitch. The corners will lie flatter if they are mitred. Now attach the fringing (see below). All the linings need to be secured in the centre of the rug to prevent them from slipping or sagging. Pin each in place in turn and secure by stab stitching along the central line lengthwise and crosswise at intervals as frequently as you feel is necessary depending on the weight of the lining and the size of the rug. Pin around the edge, turning in the lining appropriately and slip stitch. Repeat if necessary with the felt and then the outer lining. There is no need to turn the felt under as it will not fray and would make too thick an edge.

FRINGING This is absolutely a matter of taste. Fringing can be omitted altogether, done in wool or cotton, and made as simple or elaborate as you like. The two rugs shown were both fringed with a strong cotton weft.

The quantity of fringing you will need can be calculated by counting the number of stitches across the width of the rug, multiplied by two and multiplied by twice the length of fringe that you intend. If you want to experiment with knotting or plaiting, you will need more.

Decide on the length of the fringing. Then cut a long piece of card with a width that is slightly larger than the length of the fringing and wind the fringing cord around the card. Cut lengthways in a straight line with a scalpel and you will have fringing all the right length.

ATTACHING THE FRINGE The basic principle is very simple. It is just like threading a luggage label. If you could fold the one thread of fringe in half and thread the loop through the edge of the canvas from back to front, you would then need only to tuck the two loose ends through the loop and pull. However, the difficulty is getting the folded thread through the canvas hole which already contains your stitching. The quickest method is to use a latch hook, passing it through from front to back, hooking the double thread and pulling it through to the front; the hook can be used to pull the two loose ends through the loop, tightening the knot by hand. If you do not have a latch hook, a needle large enough to take the double thread will do, but it is not as quick. If you make the fringe by threading in the other direction, you will find that, from the front, you have two straight pieces of fringing with no joining loop at the top – this, too, is a matter of personal taste.

Knotting fringes can be extremely complex and great fun – but you will need a different book!

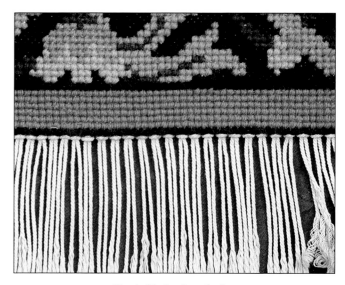

Simple fringing from the front

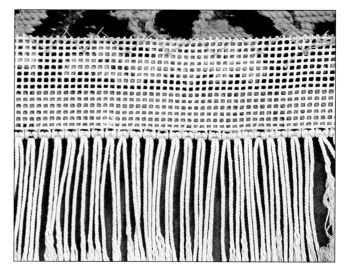

Simple fringing from the back

Slightly more complex fringing

WHERE TO BUY
KITS AND MATERIALS

Many of the following shops stock Appleton wools, DMC and Danish Flower threads, canvas, linen and other needle-point materials. Some will provide mail order, stretching and making-up services – please contact them to confirm. They are listed by districts for your convenience.

The necessary materials to stitch most of the designs in this book are also available by mail from Designers Forum, who will be pleased to send you a colour brochure and price list of these and a wide range of other complete kits based on designs from the Arts & Crafts Movement. Most of them are available with an accurately printed canvas for those who prefer not to count from a chart. For further details, write to: Designers Forum, PO Box 565, London SW1V 3PU.

BERKSHIRE
Crown Needlework, 115 High Street, Hungerford, RG17 0LU

BUCKINGHAMSHIRE
Threads of Amersham, 71 Woodside Road, Amersham on the Hill, HP6 6AA

CHESHIRE
Embroidery & Tapestry House, 32-34 Watergate Street, Chester, CH1 2LA
Voirrey Embroidery Centre, Brimstage Hall, Brimstage, Wirral, L63 6JA

CUMBRIA
Russells Needlework, 30 Castle Street, Carlisle, CA3 8TP

DERBYSHIRE
Wye Needlecraft, 2 Royal Oak Place, Matlock Street, Bakewell, DE45 1HD

DORSET
Lady Penelope, 8 Station Road, Parkstone, Poole, BH14 8UB
Sherborne Tapestry Centre, 1 Cheap Street, Sherborne, DT9 3PT

GLOUCESTERSHIRE
Campden Needlecraft Centre, High Street, Chipping Campden, GL55 6AG
Cirencester Needlecrafts, 7 Swan Yard, 13-16 West Market Place, Cirencester, GL7 2NH
Ladies Work Society, Delabere House, Moreton in Marsh, GL56 0AS

HAMPSHIRE
Tapestry Centre, 42 West Street, Alresford, SO24 9AU

HEREFORDSHIRE
Doughty Bros, 33 Church Street, Hereford, HR1 2LR

LEICESTERSHIRE
Quilts & Crafts, 4 Allandale Road, Stoneygate, Leicester, LE2 2DA

LINCOLNSHIRE
Hemsleys, 46 Steep Hill, Lincoln, LN2 1LU

LONDON
Harrods, Knightsbridge, SW1X 7XL
John Lewis, Oxford Street, W1A 1EX
Liberty, Regent Street, W1R 6AH
Peter Jones, Sloane Square, SW1W 8EL

NORFOLK
Butchers, Swan Lane, Norwich, NR2 1AP

OXFORDSHIRE
Burford Needlecraft, 117 High Street, Burford, OX18 4RG

SHROPSHIRE
House of Needlework, 11 Wyle Cop, Shrewsbury, SY1 1XB

SURREY
Pandora, 196 High Street, Guildford, GU1 3HZ

SUSSEX
David's Needleart, 37 Tarrant Street, Arundel, BN18 9DG

Needlecraft, 2A Crane Street, Chichester, PO19 1LH
Sussex Crafts, 45 High Street, Cuckfield, RH17 5JU

WILTSHIRE
Mace & Nairn, 89 Crane Street, Salisbury, SP1 2PY
Needlecraft Centre, Stable Courtyard, Longleat,
Warminster, BA12 7NL

YORKSHIRE
Ancient & Modern Tapestries, The Old Post Office, 39
Duke Street, Settle, BD24 9DJ
Craft Basics, 9 Gillygate, York, YO31 7EA
Petit Point, 12 Montpellier Parade, Harrogate, HG1 2TJ
Tapestry Garden, 2 Castlegate, Helmsley, YO62 5AB
The Viking Loom, 22 High Petergate, York, YO1 7EH

SCOTLAND
Jenners, 48 Princes Street, Edinburgh, EH2 2YJ
Christine Riley, 53 Barclay Street, Stonehaven,
Kincardineshire, AB3 2AR

EIRE
Needle Craft, 27-28 Dawson Street, Dublin 2

THE JOHN LEWIS PARTNERSHIP
Beth Russell/Designers Forum kits are available in over 20
stores throughout the UK. Call 0171 629 7711 for your
nearest store.

Further information:
APPLETON YARNS
Appleton Bros Limited, Thames Works, Church Street,
Chiswick, London, W4 2PE

DANISH FLOWER THREADS
Tapestry Centre, 42 West Street, Alresford, Hampshire,
SO24 9AU

DMC THREADS
DMC Creative World, Pullman Road, Wigston,
Leicestershire, LE8 2DY

Other good needlepoint sources (particularly for Designers
Forum kits):
AUSTRALIA
Cottage Crafts, 462 Fullarton Road, Myrtle Bank, SA 5064
The Crewel Gobelin, 5 Marian Street, Killara, NSW 2071
Mosman Needlecraft, Shop 11, 1 Mandolong Road,
Mosman, NSW 2088

Needleworld, 109D King William Road, Hyde Park, SA
5061
Petit Point, Shop 19, Yorktown Square, Launceston,
Tasmania 7250
Priscilla's Tapestry, 1205 High Street, Malvern, VIC 3144
The Silver Thimble, 204 Hay Street, Subiaco, WA 6009
Stadia Handcrafts, 85 Elizabeth Street, Paddington, NSW
2021
Tapestry Craft, 32 York Street, Sydney, NSW 2000
Victoria House Needlecraft, Hume Highway, Mittagong,
NSW 2575

BELGIUM
A la Fileuse, 25 Rue des Pierres, 1000 Brussels

CANADA
Dick & Jane, 3598 West 4th Avenue, Vancouver, BC V6R
1N8
Pointers, 99 Yorkville Avenue, Unit 103, Toronto, Ontario
M5R 3K5

FRANCE
Voisine, 12 Rue de l'Eglise, 92200 Neuilly-sur-Seine

GERMANY
Stitches, Dabringhauser Strasse 20, 42929 Wermelskirchen

ITALY
Canevas Folies, 27 Rue du Nant, CH-1207 Genève

JAPAN
Yamanashi Hemslojd, 4-3-16 Jingumae, Shibuya-ku, Tokyo
150-0001

NEW ZEALAND
Broomfields, 211 Papanui Road, Merivale, Christchurch
The Embroiderer, 140 Hinemoa Street, Birkenhead,
Auckland 1310
Nancy's Embroidery, 273 Tinakori Road, Thorndon,
Wellington

SPAIN
Bimbi, Hermosilla 49, 28001 Madrid

SWITZERLAND
Canevas Folies, 27 Rue du Nant, CH-1207 Genève

USA
Rose Cottage West, 209 Richmond Street, El Segundo, CA
90245
Potpourri Etc., 275 Church Street, Chillicothe, OH 45601

PLACES TO VISIT

Original works from the Arts & Crafts Movement are housed in the following places. Many are public museums or galleries with regular opening times. Others are collections either in the care of official bodies (such as the National Trust, the Society of Antiquaries and the Richmond Fellowship) or in private homes; these are only viewable on special dates or by written appointment.

BEDFORD — Cecil Higgins Museum
BEXLEYHEATH — Red House
BIRMINGHAM — City Museum & Art Gallery
BRISTOL — Museum & Art Gallery
CAMBRIDGE — Fitzwilliam Museum
CAMBRIDGE — Jesus College
CAMBRIDGE — Queen's College
CARDIFF — Welsh Folk Museum
CARDIFF — Castle
CHELTENHAM — Art Gallery and Museums
EAST GRINSTEAD — Standen
HARTLEBURY CASTLE — Hereford & Worcester County Museum
IRONBRIDGE — Jackfield Tile Museum

LECHLADE — Kelmscott Manor
LEICESTER — County Museum & Art Gallery
LONDON — (Hammersmith) Kelmscott House★
LONDON — (Kensington) 8 Addison Road
LONDON — (Kensington) Leighton House
LONDON (Kensington) Linley Sambourne House
LONDON — (Kensington) Victoria & Albert Museum
LONDON — (Walthamstow) William Morris Gallery
MANCHESTER — Whitworth Art Gallery
NORWICH — Castle Museum
OXFORD — Oxford Union
SWANSEA — Brangwyn Hall
UXBRIDGE — Arthur Sanderson (Archive)
WOLVERHAMPTON — Wightwick Manor

★ Kelmscott House is the headquarters of the William Morris Society, which has an active programme of lectures, visits, study days and social events, as well as a newsletter and journal. Membership applications should be addressed to Kelmscott House, 26 Upper Mall, Hammersmith, London W6 9TA.

BIBLIOGRAPHY

Adburgham, Alison *Liberty's – A Biography of a Shop* (George Allen & Unwin, 1975)

Anscombe, Isabelle *Arts and Crafts Style* (Phaidon Oxford, 1991)

Anscombe, Isabelle & Charlotte Gere *Arts and Crafts in Britain and America* (Academy Editions, 1978)

Austwick, J & B *The Decorated Tile* (Pitman House, 1980)

Catleugh, Jon *William De Morgan Tiles* (Trefoil Books, 1983)

Clark, Fiona *William Morris – Wallpapers and Chintzes* (St Martin's Press/Academy Editions, 1973)

Coote, Stephen *William Morris – His Life and Work* (Garamond, 1990)

Dore, Helen *William Morris* (Pyramid Books, 1990)

Durant, Stuart *The Decorative Designs of C.F.A. Voysey* (The Lutterworth Press, 1990)

Fairclough, Oliver & Emmeline Leary *Textiles by William Morris and Morris & Co 1861–1940* (Thames and Hudson, 1981)

Gillow, Norah *William Morris – Designs and Patterns* (Bracken Books, 1988)

Greenwood, Martin *The Designs of William De Morgan* (Dennis and Wiltshire, 1989)

MacCarthy, Fiona *William Morris, A Life for Our Time* (Faber & Faber, 1994)

Naylor, Gillian *The Arts & Crafts Movement* (Studio Vista, 1980)

Naylor, Gillian *William Morris By Himself* (Macdonald Orbis, 1988)

Parry, Linda *Textiles of the Arts & Crafts Movement* (Thames & Hudson, 1988)

Parry, Linda *William Morris* (Philip Wilson, in association with the Victoria & Albert Museum, 1996)

Parry, Linda *William Morris and the Arts & Crafts Movement* (Studio Editions, 1989)

Parry, Linda *William Morris Textiles* (Weidenfield & Nicolson, 1983)

Poulson, Christine *William Morris* (Apple Press, 1989)

Vallance, Aymer *The Art of William Morris* (Dover, 1990)

Vallance, Aymer *The Life and Work of William Morris* Studio Editions, 1986)

Watkinson, Ray *William Morris as Designer* (Studio Vista, 1967)

Wilhide, Elizabeth *William Morris – Design and Decor* (Pavilion, 1991)

ACKNOWLEDGEMENTS

To acknowledge fully all the help that I have had in producing this book is impossible. There are, however, many people who deserve special mention, often for performing even more roles than they were originally asked to fulfil.

My husband, Peter, not only gave me confidence and advice but together with the rest of our family – particularly Nick, Paul and Julie – allowed me the time and space that I needed by keeping Designers Forum alive and well. Thanks, also, to daughter-in-law Sam and my brother Roy Haynes for constant encouragement. Plus Appleton Bros for their usual colourful service . . . Simon Deighton for his excellent and reliable printing . . . Sheila Thom for making tidiness out of chaos . . . Jean and Frank Dittrich in California and Lawton Cooke in Australia for continuous support . . . they all enabled the business to carry on without me.

The finished pieces in the book would not be there without the artistic abilities of Phyllis and Robert Steed and the superb stitching of Selina Winter, Angela Kahan, Jean Cook, Lesley Paddon and Dorothy Vernon.

The genuinely pretty, as well as practical, charts demonstrate the technical skills of Ethan Danielson; Maggi McCormick deserves special appreciation for wrestling so tactfully with my verbal ramblings; Brenda Morrison is responsible for the elegant design of the whole book. The beautiful photographs are due to the skill of John Greenwood. His understanding of my work and his constant enthusiasm have made the hunting for locations and the photographic sessions great fun. He and I were helped in no small way by the styling of Andrea Spencer, Kes Seeberg and Dilys Williams, and by the good humour and imagination of his assistant, Quentin Harriott.

For the loan of their homes, furniture or props, I should like to thank Michael and Gaynor Wilson, Oliver and his parents, Caroline Perry at The Tapestry Centre, Jane Chapman of Campden Needlecraft, John Masterson, Mikiko Yamanashi and Jean Wells. For special locations and loan of photographs, my thanks to Linda Howarth of The Richmond Fellowship (8 Addison Road), Matthew Wise of Markheath Securities (Stanmore Hall), Norah Gillow at The William Morris Gallery and, at Arthur Sanderson & Sons, Lesley Hoskins at the Archive and Elizabeth Machin in the Press Office.

Finally, I acknowledge the patience of Vivienne Wells at David & Charles; her faith in me is more appreciated than she knows.

Many of the individuals that I have mentioned are now personal friends; that is the pleasure and privilege of working with talented people. I want to thank them all for their inspiration and enthusiasm.

*The highly individual and untutored
efforts of my husband in 1973!*

INDEX

40/423/2